Innovating IT: Transforming IT from Cost Crunchers to Growth Drivers

Innovating IT: Transforming IT from Cost Crunchers to Growth Drivers

Lior Arussy

Wiley Publishing, Inc.

Vice President & Executive Group Publisher: Richard Swadley
Publisher: Joe Wikert
Acquisitions Editor: Katie Mohr
Development Editor and Copy Editor: Rebecca Whitney
Senior Development Editor: Kevin Kent
Editorial Manager: Mary Beth Wakefield
Senior Production Editor: Angela Smith
Project Coordinator: April Farling
Text Design & Composition: Wiley Composition Services

Published by
Wiley Publishing, Inc.
10475 Crosspoint Boulevard
Indianapolis, IN 46256
www.wiley.com

Copyright © 2005 by Lior Arussy
Published by Wiley Publishing, Inc., Indianapolis, Indiana
Published simultaneously in Canada
ISBN: 0-7645-8369-7
Manufactured in the United States of America
10 9 8 7 6 5 4 3 2 1
1C/QT/RS/QU/IN

To My Family with Love

Acknowledgments

Many people contributed to this book with their insight, ideas, and overall support. I would like to express my deep appreciation to them because without them, this book would never have seen the light of day: Andy Mulholland, Bill Mann, Dan Woods, Eli Gorovici, Giddy Hollander, Jackie Smith, Jason Wolf, Jeroen Tas, Lina Librety, Lloyd Wilke, Ori Inbar, Peter Graf, Ron Moritz, Russ Arts, Scott Feldman, Shelli Weisz, Toby Weiss, Tom Pfister, Tom Weisz, Tsvi Gal, Russell M. Artzt, and Ilona Mohacsi.

Special thanks to Rachel Yurowitz, for her editorial insight and making sure that every *i* is dotted and every *t* is crossed. Special thanks to the Wiley Publishing team, including Katie Mohr, Rebecca Whitney, Kevin Kent, Angela Smith, April Farling, and all the others at Wiley who had a hand in helping bring this book together.

To my family, who again needed to endure another passionate outburst. I love you and appreciate the privilege of your love. Thank God.

Contents

x *Contents*

Introduction

The technology world has undergone some sharp changes in the past two decades. New technologies have changed the foundations of traditional companies and industries and given birth to fresh ones. Markets and industries have undergone a fundamental transformation caused by technological advances. Many argue that these changes are no different from other innovative ideas that transformed the world, such as the change from railroads to aviation and from the telegraph to the cellular phone. From their origin as a competitive advantage, technologies quickly dissolved into invisible commodities, thus adding new recognizable value, so the argument goes.

Although the argument has some truth to it, it misses a major differentiator that applies to the progress of technologies and their business impact. Technologies are now at a crossroads, subject to multiple trends that threaten their existence as we know it. From outsourcing to users ignoring the growing masses of information presented to them, and from budget and power shifts in business units to unrealized return on investment, IT operations are at a critical juncture. IT organizations must decide who they are, what their role is, and how they can contribute while the pace of technology commoditization is accelerating.

IT operations that merely focus on managing infrastructure, which now consumes an average of 80 percent of their budgets, are blind to the rising challenge. How do they connect to the core of their businesses? How do they drive top-line business growth and not just bottom-line cost reduction? Well positioned and measured in terms of cost reduction, IT is often not regarded by executives as something that drives revenue or enables growth. These executives' view of the IT cost-crunching role has become a self-fulfilling prophecy. IT has not been invited to assist in revenue generation, innovation, or growth. It is this combination of cost crunching and infrastructure focus that has led to the current challenge for IT to redefine itself.

To connect to the core agenda of the CEO, IT personnel must evolve to become innovation drivers and to assist in the growth engines of their organizations. The first order of business for IT must be to focus on users, by redesigning their experience to enhance information utilization. IT will then make a positive contribution to decision making and the innovation cycle. This shift requires a redefinition of core competencies as well as changes in priorities and resource allocation. This concept is not a slogan—it requires an operational approach and detailed execution.

TECHNOLOGY—ITS PRODUCT INFORMATION AND ITS PRACTITIONERS

IT professionals have a major void to fill in helping their organizations adopt a systematic mechanism for innovation. The tools and information they use can, and must, play a role in accelerating change and driving user decisions and risk management. The opportunity is there; IT professionals must embrace the challenge and transform themselves into information managers and enablers of innovation. As with any other change, trade-offs and adaptation are required. However, the reward for both IT and the entire organization justifies, if not surpasses, the required effort. Although cost reduction may be a short-term strategy, winning companies are betting on growth and innovation as a long-term strategy. By adapting to and enabling innovation, IT is in a position to take a long-term role that makes a lasting impact. Rather than focus on system legacy, it facilitates a people legacy.

This book is a journey of change, from the self-centered capabilities of managing servers and storage tools to a user-centric approach that drives innovation through information utilization. It is an agenda of changing IT activities from being technology-centric, where users are secondary to processes and technologies, to an IT organization that starts with its users and then adapts tools and information for delivery to those users based on their usage, business impact, and consumption behavior. This situation represents a transformation from the popular mode of information production, where users are responsible for using it, to information utilization, where IT is responsible for user utilization and is measured by its impact. This information technology operation is transformed into individual technology, which then leads to innovation technology.

1

IT, an Industry at a Crossroads: Current Trends and Future Impact

"Progress is impossible without change, and those who cannot change their minds can not change anything"

George Bernard Shaw

THE INHERENT CONFLICT EXPLORED

A large telecom provider in the United States recently issued new guidelines for technology purchasing. The company now requires that all technology acquisitions bring a return on investment in fewer than 12 months and also justify head count reduction. As one vendor pitched a new technology for purchase, it adhered to the guidelines and prepared a complete justification model that met both conditions. After the case was presented to the company's top operations executives, the proposal was rejected immediately. The reason: "We cannot afford another single layoff. We need the people."

For the past several years, IT has played the role of cost reducer. Originally, cost reduction was only one dimension of the overall technology justification. However, in the past few years, it has taken the driver's seat. Technology was used as a means to optimize processes and ultimately justify cost reduction. Today, however, this role of technology as a cost cruncher is a major obstacle in its own ability to connect to the business's strategic objectives.

> " Today, however, this role of technology as a cost cruncher is a major obstacle in its own ability to connect to the business's strategic objectives. "

Overexploitation of cost reduction combined with overpromised savings is a primary reason for the pendulum shift that affects the IT role today. Another reason is the CEO's renewed optimism that the organization is back on the growth track. A recent IBM study of CEOs identified growth as the key initiative and focus of their organizations. However, only 4 percent of the surveyed CEOs regarded IT as a contributor to growth and innovation.

The IT function in large organizations is at a crossroads (see Figure 1-1). With the growing popularity of outsourcing and co-sourcing, many IT professionals are finding themselves in a tough spot. Our estimates show that more than 500,000 individuals are working in companies with outsourcing as a core value proposition.

The growth in outsourcing is fueled by two major drivers:

- The notion that IT is not essential to the business and, as such, can be given to outside sources to manage more effectively, just like the electrical network and sewer system. By doing so, a leverage of economies of scale is achieved by pooling the strength of multiple organizational requirements.
- The assumption that IT is a true commodity, equal to paper clips and staplers, and has no specific relevance to a certain organization or industry. By focusing on cost reduction, this driver is leading the company to outside sources to further achieve cost reductions that could not be achieved internally. This flawed line of thinking views IT from a narrow prism of plumbing and servers and fails to see the potential of IT in the innovation cycle of the organization.

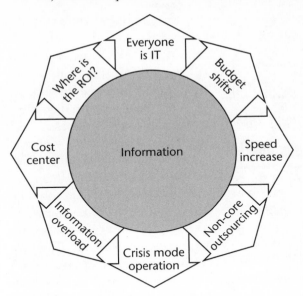

Figure 1-1. IT at a Crossroads

Imagine half a million people pointing at you and claiming that they can do your job better and faster somewhere else. This thought is not a flattering one. It is, however, the core of the outsourcing message and value proposition today. More and more IT professionals are in an ambiguous, conflicting relationship with the outsourcing concept. On one hand, they realize that they need outsourcers. On the other hand, they are uncertain of the scope of the threat. Add to the mix the increased volume of information available to users, and the result is confusion and the inability to use the wealth of information produced in their organizations.

"In the past, I led innovation; today, I am being led by innovation." I heard this statement from the CIO of a major American entertainment company who explained to me that technology budgets and the responsibility for them are quickly shifting toward the business units and their users, thus diminishing the role of IT. Following years of making technology user friendly and assisting users to become more technologically savvy, IT is now facing a new user approach to technology. In a world where every user operates a home PC, plays Playstation 2, and is wirelessly connected to the Web, the strong belief is that all users have mastered the art of technology management. This evolving attitude, fueled by a new generation of younger employees who are comfortable with technology, poses a greater risk to the integrity and success of IT in the corporate world.

> " In the past, I led innovation; today, I am being led by innovation. "

Younger, technology-savvy employees are purchasing and installing their own software. Business units are making independent decisions and implementing whatever solutions they require. Both often bypass the IT function altogether or reduce its role to a consultative one. Software and tools are continually being downloaded by users without IT permission or knowledge. Overall, there is a growing conviction of the IT function's diminishing value. This trend is validated by the numbers. A 2003 study conducted by *Network Computing* magazine revealed that less than 50 percent of the budgets for IT projects are in the hands of IT. This represents a major shift from a decade ago, when IT controlled the vast majority of technology budgets. The user friendliness of technology has led many users to believe that they are capable of making technology decisions and purchases on their own and bypassing their IT departments. In these cases, IT has been demoted to the role of corporate police, to merely ensure compatibility with corporate guidelines.

The challenge of return on investment (ROI) is another element influencing the future of IT. IT is regarded as a cost center. Ask any CFO whether she truly reduces the budget line item as per the ROI analysis presented to justify the technology project of the day, and the high likelihood is that the answer will be "No." In many organizations where IT is still a cost center and no accountability has been put in place to hold users and business units responsible and accountable for their technology choices, IT represents a bottomless pit of ongoing spending. The CIO of a leading entertainment company mentioned that, in the past, his company ran 30 major IT projects every year. Of these, only 5 or 6 projects were considered successful while the rest died a slow and painful death. When asked whether true ROI accountability had been put in place, he said that the business units that initiated many of the IT projects were reluctant to commit to the savings indicated in the initial project justification.

When the CFO finally required that every declared savings be realized from the business units' budgets and that the units would be held accountable, the response was a sharp decline in project requests. Today, the company initiates five or six projects a year, but they are all reaching successful implementation. In a sense, by not holding its customers responsible and accountable, IT allowed the ongoing abuse of its own resources and by doing so caused some of its current challenges.

CLOUDS, ARROWS, AND SPAGHETTI

One anecdotal, yet strong, testimonial for IT's distancing itself from its users is the "famous" network architecture example. Have you ever visited a conference room at the conclusion of an IT meeting? You would most likely stand there staring at the whiteboard and scratching your head. The board is covered with drawings of clouds, arrows, and boxes. In part of the diagram, the arrows are transformed into lightning-like arrows that connect some of the clouds to some boxes. Another variation of the unique IT artistic phenomena on the whiteboard has curvy lines seemingly connecting boxes to create a puzzling picture of spaghetti; you cannot comprehend where it starts and where it is going. Words rarely accompany this abstract art. Explanations are out of the question. In this closed club, if you don't get it, you don't belong.

There is one surprising aspect of those network diagrams and the architecture depicting networks connections, applications, and servers: You do not see even one picture of a user. Users are not part of the picture. The total focus of IT on its own wares neglects to include users in the overall picture. In rare cases, users are represented by pictures of smaller boxes, symbolizing desktop computers. Again, users are viewed from the perspective of the wares, not as stand-alone living beings with individual needs and requirements. Depicting users as desktops represents the mindset that they are subservient to the process or architecture, not primary to it.

This mindset, which most IT professionals would deny, is at the core of their challenging transformations. Recognizing the absence of users from their pictures is the first step. Including users as primary, not secondary, to the architecture is the critical step shown in Figure 1-2. At the core of this transformation is recognizing that networks, connections, and clouds, although important, are not the core competency of the future. The core competency is servicing users.

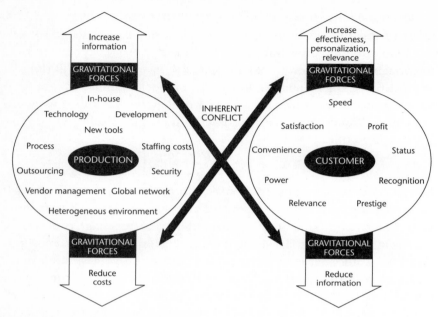

Figure 1-2.   The Inherent Conflict

In examining the typical IT function, you can see that it resides in an ecosystem of issues and concerns. This ecosystem, which includes the cost of management, outsourcing issues, a global network infrastructure, and security are some of the everyday crisis mode matters that occupy the daily routine of the CIO and his staff. These are the functional requirements for running an effective IT operation. They are the issues that dictate the agenda and the resources of the IT operation. The two gravitational forces that pull this ecosystem in two inherently conflicting directions are reducing costs and producing more information. The assumption is that the more information that is produced, the more productive employees are.

This IT ecosystem and its gravitational forces dictate the agenda and focus of the IT function. On average, 80 percent of its resources and budget are tied to basic infrastructure requirements, such as server hardware, network tools, desktop hardware, and security solutions.

With such heavy financial investment and management attention, it is no wonder that the customer's ecosystem is ignored. None of the IT ecosystem components is part of the customer ecosystem. The customer focuses on her own success factors and seeks prestige, promotion, and the fast and convenient execution of tasks. The two diametrically opposed gravitational forces pulling the customer ecosystem are the need for more personally relevant information and the reduction of information cost.

In examining both ecosystems, it is clear why IT is missing the mark on the organization's latest agenda. Living in their own world of the production of information, IT professionals fail to see, measure, and execute information utilization. By being concerned with cost reduction, they produce masses of information

> *" Living in their own world of the production of information, IT professionals fail to see, measure, and execute information utilization. "*

that are, by definition, less relevant to their customers. Bombarded with growing quantities of information, customers reach the turning point of being unable to consume and utilize the information provided.

Lacking the traditional accountability of product and utilization, this inherent conflict between provider and customer was allowed to fester for many years. Recently, in the name of self service, IT placed on web portals and intranets the information it produced and pushed the responsibility of searching for the relevant information to its customers. The customers, facing a larger pool of information from which to search, opted out and ignored altogether the information produced.

COST CUTTING: THE SHORT-TERM STRATEGY

The cost-cutting measures in which IT played a major role over the past few years created a rigid system unwilling to adapt to evolving user needs. When an organization lacks innovation, it focuses on cost reduction. Because growth and innovation are often perceived as unpredictable, cost reduction became the comfortable choice. In the name of digitization and automation, IT and its technology were primarily positioned for cost reduction. This positioning allowed for better justification of the proposed technology investment because no executive was willing to commit to top-line growth. Head count reduction and the cancellation of functions were the typical results of IT projects. Although savings were accrued, they came with a price. User resentment toward IT and a lack of association with innovation prevailed. IT won the conspicuous title of a necessary evil with rigid systems as opposed to being enablers and business drivers. This image put the relationship between IT and its users on the wrong foot.

Users, increasingly operating in crisis mode, find the IT systems unhelpful and unsupportive of their evolving needs. This crisis mode of operation affected IT and shifted its focus to incremental impact projects. It also delayed investment in innovation supporting infrastructure, which is so desperately needed for a fast-changing environment. By reacting to isolated requests from users and creating homegrown applications, IT populated their environments with hundreds of applications and information sources that require expensive maintenance and as such moved their organizations backward. The sense of "the more, the merrier" made IT professionals believe that the larger the number of applications they manage, the stronger and more indispensable they are in the organization. This information-production attitude must change if they ever want to leap toward the mainstream of the business.

> " *IT won the conspicuous title of a necessary evil with rigid systems as opposed to being enablers and business drivers.* "

Now, facing multiple patched systems, each addressing one type of problem with expensive connectors to the other systems, the IT landscape looks more like a collection of patchwork components. This moved the organization years backward as the cost of maintenance and information searches became prohibitive. As opposed to a beautiful interwoven fabric where each color enhances the value of the overall carpet, IT looks more like a mixture of chemical liquids that do not mix well to create a workable solution.

The cost-cutting focus of many IT organizations and their companies dealt a devastating blow to their readiness for innovation and growth. In fact, it placed them in a less competitive position vis-a-vis newcomers in their industry. Lacking flexible tools for innovation while maintaining and managing patch-based systems severely limits information availability and makes it cost prohibitive. In addition, the legacy patchwork system set IT and its organizations back several years as it increased the overall costs of maintenance and reduced the funds available to address the needs of innovation and growth. Any competing start-up company in the market space is better positioned to compete. Without the costs and complexity of a patchwork-based legacy environment, the company can quickly adapt to market needs and create cost-effective innovative solutions that drive growth. The legacy patch-work company, on the other hand, faces hurdles because of its legacy and is most likely unable to match the price competitiveness of the start-up because of these maintenance costs. In an environment where speed, agility, and the ability to deliver solutions with a better cost structure are crucial to success, patch-based legacies are a significant hurdle to not only IT success but also overall business success.

WHERE IS THE INFORMATION?

Another major byproduct of the legacy patch system is the inability to access information because of the inability to know what information exists and where it is. Accessing information becomes an increasingly difficult and time-consuming task. Because of inconsistent information formats across the various applications, users do not even know what to search for and how to define their searches. This hurdle decreases information utilization and therefore increases the cost of information.

Users with less time to spend on information access now face contradictory drivers where the more applications and sources of information are in their organizations, the less transparent the information is. A direct correlation exists between the amount of available information and information utilization. Because users do not know what information is available and where it can be found, these drivers significantly reduce the utilization of event-critical information that can and should be used to avoid mistakes, mitigate risks, and maximize opportunities. The result is devastating. Information production costs are assumed by organizations, but utilization and impact on the business are minimized.

USER ACCESS AND MISMANAGEMENT

Another important byproduct of the legacy patch system is that a unique access and user privilege management system is required by every application. They are often conflicting and inconsistent from a business standpoint. Legitimate users are not granted access to the information they so critically need, and unauthorized users somehow get their hands on information they should not see. Often, access to each

> " Legitimate users are not granted access to the information they so critically need, and unauthorized users somehow get their hands on information they should not see. "

application is managed by a different owner within IT. Users need to follow a tortuous process to obtain access to the information they need in order to run their businesses.

The cost of maintaining access and user privileges to all these applications is prohibitive as well. These costs include the direct cost of IT personnel time to manage the application and the indirect cost of not having access to critical information, delays in access, and access provided to employees who have left the company and might be working for the competition. In some situations, employees who have left a company still have access to confidential and competitive information 30 to 60 days after leaving, simply because the person managing the application did not "get around to" removing them. The cost of this unauthorized access is immeasurable.

Considering the frequent reorganization programs that can change as often as monthly, user access and the ability to quickly assume new roles are crucial to business success. Again, IT becomes the obstacle, not the accelerator, by not granting users immediate access to the information they need.

By assuming a production-centric view, IT did not adopt the overall user perspective and did not design its services and access to information to follow user behavior and experience. That mistaken assumption has tremendous costs associated with it.

INFORMATION OVERFLOW: NOW WHAT?

Faced with too much information, users opt to use none. While recently searching for a digital camera on the Web, I came across more than 1,500 options and alternatives. With such a huge selection, users have no way to apply logical criteria to make reasonable decisions. Users have neither the time nor the knowledge to process all the required information in order to make informed decisions. Such a huge selection creates the turning point that makes users opt out. They simply neglect all the options and free themselves from the burden of dealing with the issues. As such, they choose to make emotional, intuitive decisions. This option might be a legitimate one for many branded products that try to lure customers on emotions only. But it is a serious failure for the producers of information, also known as IT operations. They cannot afford the luxury of their product—information—being so blatantly ignored. The larger-than-ever information pool created by corporations does not drive more control over the business, but, rather, drives confusion.

One emerging technology is RFID, the tiny identification device that allows optimal inventory management. It brings with it the ability to track items in real time at any part of the supply chain and to optimize inventory and sales as a result. This technology is bound to add a significant information load on its already information-ridden users. This additional information is being heralded with many benefits to every business. Companies will enjoy a new source of knowledge that empowers them to manage their products better and more profitably, the promise states. Like any other emerging new source of technology, placed in isolation, the information is being positioned with a critical "How could we conduct business without it?" attitude. But when RFID—or any other emerging source of information, for that matter—is placed in the context of the existing growing load of information facing users, it bears some serious challenges as well. Unless managed and delivered in a different and efficient way, this additional dimension of information is destined to join the already piling amount of information that users view as impossible to deal with. Limited by time, resources, and a decision-making timeframe, users are likely to see little if any benefit from the additional information delivered through RFID.

> **" Companies will enjoy a new source of knowledge that empowers them to manage their products better and more profitably, the promise states. "**

Users' experiences with information have always been constrained because of their emotional decision making. Overwhelming amounts of information simply push users over the edge and prevent usage altogether or lower it to marginal, insignificant decisions.

SPEED AND ITS IMPACT ON INFORMATION UTILIZATION

Users today have less time to make decisions. They must form opinions and reach conclusions at a faster pace. Products and services must be introduced faster than ever, and any function that plays a role in delaying those crucial decisions is marginalized. Years of rigid processes turned IT into one of those functions that stands in the way of organizations and their need for speed. Like other basic needs, this one will never be completely addressed, but probably will become more demanding as it evolves. IT systems are not built for moving targets, but, rather, for well-defined and predictable requirements. This greater lack of predictability experienced by users is forcing IT to play a lesser role in an organization's most critical decisions. No executive has enough time to wait for information. Competitive forces are challenging him to respond fast, so his attitude is clear: "No excuses. Either you are on my side, or you are against me." IT has failed to be on the executives' side because of the inherent limitations in their systems and information delivery.

With these pressures affecting the role of IT, its function is at a crossroads. It should be no surprise that in a recent study by *CIO* magazine, 18 percent of CIOs indicated that they expect their jobs to be eliminated in the next five years. This statistic should not be surprising, considering the preceding factors that affect the IT function. Lacking a future vision and fearing the unknown rather

> **" IT must redefine itself and its role in the organization or face its inevitable fate. "**

than embracing it and building a roadmap for it, is the reason that many CIOs see their function and responsibilities evaporating. This lack of vision and roadmap results in timid IT attempts to survive the pressuring drivers, hoping that they will lessen as the economy gets better. In reality, they are not likely to lessen. After getting used to IT personnel as cost crunchers, CFOs are less likely to regress to the old system of technology spending. IT must redefine itself and its role in the organization or face its inevitable fate. The challenge lies squarely on IT to reinvent itself and become an integral, crucial contributor to the business.

2

From Information Production to Information Utilization

Unused knowledge is irresponsibility.

LA

THE EVOLUTION OF INFORMATION

The evolution of information in every organization is a story of a learning curve, risk, and confidence (see Figure 2-1). Whenever a new organization is formed or a new product created, the amount of information available to make decisions is quite limited.

At the idea stage, launching an idea requires a high degree of change and risk. When the idea reaches some level of market acceptance, the organization moves to the next stage.

The innovation stage allows organizations to listen to market needs and respond to incremental customer requirements, which fine-tunes the product or service for mass-market acceptance.

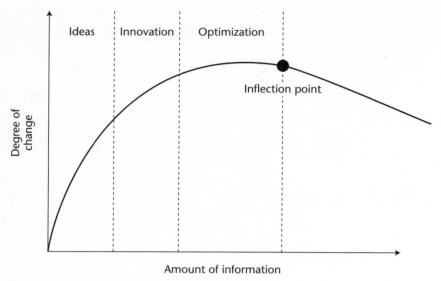

Figure 2-1.   The Evolution of Information

By the time the product or service reaches mass-market acceptance, the organization has generated a significant amount of information that steers it to the optimization stage. At this stage, the company is no longer in product innovation, but is instead searching for ways to make its production more cost effective and to reduce the cost of goods and sales. It is, overall, conducting business. It is at the optimization stage that the company faces a real challenge. At this stage, the company has a strong sense of control over the initial idea and a very low degree of change. It then can focus consistency and cost reduction.

The amount of information generated is significant and often leads to a false sense of security, which results in complacency. The information is then misused. Rather than provide guidance for growth, it serves as a tool for delaying change. Companies that reach the inflection point, which is part of the optimization stage, often miss the mark and stick to the information as a shield from change and disruption. Rather than use the amount of information they have acquired for their next big idea, companies prefer to follow the beaten path, by sticking to the original idea and fearing any change or reinvention.

Information is misused to reiterate the organization's position and rid it of the paranoia of competition. The sense of success supported by hard information leads organizations to rest on their laurels and assume that whatever happened in the past will repeat itself in the future. They believe that they have the information to prove it. With this attitude, these companies usually leave it to start-ups, which treat the inflection point in the market differently, to reinvent the product or service, much to the surprise of the large, established industry players.

> " *Rather than use the amount of information they have acquired for their next big idea, companies prefer to follow the beaten path, by sticking to the original idea and fearing any change or reinvention.* "

INFORMATION USAGE EVOLUTION

The information available in an organization is first used to discover what is going on in the organization. Transforming the organization from chaos to order is the first priority while the idea is taking shape. Business leaders then seek control over the business and better insight into the dynamics leading their newly introduced idea (see Figure 2-2).

Following the discovery stage, information moves to the next stage: Reiterate the existing operation. Ensuring consistency is the new objective as the business evolves into the mass market and requires a more organized operation. After the business's leaders gain better insight into their business, they move swiftly to create consistent processes to ensure competitive positioning and the ability to deal with growing demand.

As processes and products are improved, information usage evolves into the optimization stage, where the information is used to improve existing processes and save costs. As new competitors evolve, many of them do not bear the original costs of introduction and market education. The company must stay competitive by reducing its costs to match its new competitors' prices.

The challenge many organizations fail to meet is evolving to the ultimate stage: Utilize the information for creating something new rather than reiterate the existing. By leveraging the significant amount of information collected, companies can then invent with lower risk and

> **" The challenge many organizations fail to meet is evolving to the ultimate stage: Utilize the information for creating something new rather than reiterate the existing. "**

disruption, although they often do not see this opportunity. The significant amount of information they have gathered ends up serving exactly the opposite purpose: It prevents, rather than supports, innovation and new ideas. Executives trust the information and interpret it as a sign of the future rather than as historic behavior. They falsely assume that the future will follow the past. Using information to reaffirm their past decisions, as opposed to instituting new ones, is a common mistake that leads companies to complacency. Information supports complacency with one seriously incorrect assumption: The future will follow the past.

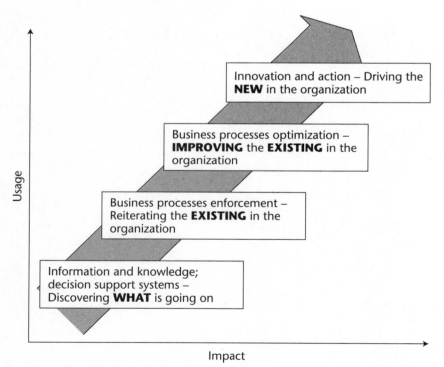

Figure 2-2.   The Evolution of Information Usage

Reinventing the new still remains, in the minds of IT professionals, the domain of the intuitive process with minimal use of existing available information. They still wait for the inspiration or the stroke of lightning to bring the next big idea, while the answer might be right under their noses, in the pile of information they labored to create through their business experience.

A NEW PRISM, A NEW ROLE

To realign the IT function with the core of the business it serves, IT executives should change the view of who they are and what they do in their organizations. The shift must start by changing the perception of IT professionals as managers of tools and infrastructure (which can be outsourced and are not a core competency of most businesses) to producers of information. Managing the corporate network is not a way to connect to the corporate mainstream focus on growth through innovation. It is merely a cost of

> " *To realign the IT function with the core of the business it serves, IT executives should change the view of who they are and what they do in their organizations.* "

doing business and equal to other basic requirements, such as buildings and utilities. As such, it is destined to be a non-essential position.

Imagine information as a product, and imagine IT professionals as sellers of that product. What is the best-selling piece of information? What is the shelf life of the information? Would it last in a competitive environment? Would customers be willing to pay for it? These are some of the critical shifts that IT personnel need to make in their understanding of their businesses.

IT measurements must adapt accordingly. Rather than focus on on-time service metrics, IT professionals must evolve to be measured on their information utilization. Did it grow or decline? Is the information exercising a 50 percent growth in usage? Do they have information products that should be discontinued because of lack of interest? What critical decisions in the organization took advantage of the information? What risk was reduced because of better information utilization? IT should evolve its view and way of measuring itself to reflect its business impact. It should not just maintain a plumbing system and say, "We deliver the infrastructure—what you do with it is your choice."

This view changes the position of IT personnel from "the people responsible for plumbing" to "the people who ensure product usage and user satisfaction." Technology executives must view their role through a prism, by looking at their products from a new perspective: information and user acceptance. They must become a combination of product (information) sellers, educators, coaches, and mentors of the usage of their products and not just be artists who glorify their tools (servers, security, and applications). As such, their focus should shift from maintaining networks to ensuring full product utilization and user satisfaction.

The two key principles of this shift are the focus on product utilization and users' experience and satisfaction. IT professionals must engage in understanding how users consume their products and what makes them relevant. Like true product managers, IT must ensure that the product is relevant and that users "buy it" and are satisfied with it. The challenge is even greater when most users take advantage of the available technology in its limited form (transactional flow automation), thus neglecting the decision support and innovation aspects of the information gathered by the technologies.

Considered and managed as a product, the role of information and how it is used in the organization changes. It is a shift from perceiving value from the perspective of system servers and tools to defining it from the perspective of user proficiency and utilization. What is the most often used piece of information? Who are the top users of information? How do they consume information? These are some of the questions that must appear on the radar screen of IT executives.

As information product managers, IT professionals should also be concerned with the following questions:

- **Who are IT professionals—information producers or information providers?** Producers care for their production conditions and facilities. Their core competency is the production aspect, and they do it in the most cost-effective way. Information and product utilization and methods that are used to deliver them to customers are out of their scope and often left to third parties or to the customers themselves to figure out. In the information stage, customers often are underutilizing the information provided, either for lack of understanding, lack of tools, lack of product availability when needed, or simply too much information that causes confusion rather than clarity.

- **Can users consume all the information that IT professionals produce?** The growing amount of information gathered and produced every day creates a conflicting situation for customers. Although customers are interested in its value and insight, when information reaches a certain mass, it becomes unusable. Today's users are at the point where IT-produced information is no longer usable because of the quantities provided. Users do not have the time and tools to process, prioritize, and make sense of the often conflicting information available. As such, information is used for minor rather than major decisions and actions. It is often used to substantiate decisions after the fact. In many cases, conflicting information supports conflict-

> **" " *Today's users are at the point where IT-produced information is no longer usable because of the quantities provided.* " "**

ing positions in an organization. This fact alone dilutes the value of information in users' eyes. If information can support conflicting decisions, its value diminishes and it becomes useless to users.

- **Are users really using the information?** This question is a matter of user behavior. It has more to do with psychology than with corporate guidelines. In fact, many users are not educated in information utilization and often misuse and abuse the available information. Their information usage declines as their confidence in their own gut feelings increases. The longer users are employed in a company, the less information they use. Veteran users develop a confidence level in their understanding of their businesses that allows them, in their minds, to bypass the available information and just use their common sense to make critical decisions.

- **How do IT professionals measure their success?** IT focuses on utility measures to examine its successes. Like an electric or telecom company, it focuses on network availability regardless of user utilization. Just like an electric company is not concerned with user utilization and what devices they use, IT does not concern itself with user activities as long as they are not illegal. The selection of these measures is directly related to these issues:

  - *The ability to meet the numbers easily and reach stated objectives.* It is simply easier to guarantee network availability than to commit to users' unpredictable behavior.

  - *The preferred shift of responsibility.* It is more convenient for IT to focus on production than to shift the responsibility to users to determine their utilization. There is no penalty for doing this and no apparent negative consequence. Although the consequences might be not apparent, however, they are quite severe.

IT is driving itself into commoditization and irrelevance in the company's mainstream growth activities. These measures of uptime and network availability are the sure path to diminishing returns and irrelevance of the organization. Just as CEOs have little concern for their companies' utility providers and take them for granted, they will not be concerned much with IT if it behaves like a utility function.

- **If the IT-produced information were available for sale as a product, what would its price be?** This question is a frightening one for many IT professionals. They are afraid of the potential answer to this question because they have never exposed themselves to market conditions or supply and demand. Having never lived in a competitive environment, they are concerned about the consequences of applying an economic model to their products and services. If users would have to pay for information, it is unclear whether they would ever buy it, what price they would be willing to pay, and under what conditions. The willingness to purchase, which indicates usage and value, is the critical indicator for the product's validity from the user's perspective. It is the application of this exact economic model that drives a true understanding of the product's value and encourages utilization. Users who determine the price also use what they pay for. When the product is free, they are free to demand more information and ignore it all. Every IT organization has numerous stories of users asking for certain information and applications, only to ignore them later. Applying an economic model and line of thinking to information drives users' accountability and utilization. It provides IT with a better way to evaluate the value for users and assign priorities and resources accordingly.

- **How would this product be packaged?** Today's preferred packaging is a self-service model that provides raw information for users to take advantage of. Some reporting and business intelligence are added to provide processing of the information. But that is where it ends. In applying the proposed economic model, packaging becomes a driver. Users might pay a certain price for self service, but be willing to double the price if the information is delivered at a greater level of analysis and compared to other, outside sources. The more processing and analysis that are provided, the higher the price. Packaging can also mean availability through mobile devices, availability through phone-based service, or speedy or real-time delivery. All are factors that are user determined and support users' total experience. The packaging, therefore, is a derivative of user requirements and their willingness to pay.

- **How would the information be sold—as a product, service, annual subscription, or results-based outcome?** "In what form would the information be sold?" is the next question in the economic model. Would it be one-time usage or a permanent license? Would it be authorized for one user or for many users? Would it be an annual sub-scription or an ongoing license? What if users would be willing to pay based only on results? When users view information as a tool, they com-mit to it only if it guarantees success. This risk-sharing model is a legiti-mate request that IT is reluctant to provide, by claiming that it has no control over user behavior and utilization. Different users have different preferences based on their engagement with the information and the importance the information plays in their overall decision-making process and their operation. This level of granularity and flexibility allows IT to deliver services and informa-tion as users want to consume them. Unlike the one-size-fits-all model of today, this level of flexibility will make information more usable and useful for users and will drive better utilization and better decisions.

> " *Unlike the one-size-fits-all model of today, this level of flexibility will make information more usable and useful for users and will drive better uti-lization and better decisions.* "

- **What is the impact on the business?** The information sold must be designed to sup-port the business. Measured around its impact on key busi-ness decisions, information must be aligned with strategies, must be able to respond to their changing nature regularly, and must stay relevant. Old information is often outdated and therefore irrelevant. IT must create evolving information platforms that allow the agility required by the business. If the business has to adopt rigid IT systems, the information will simply be ignored. As with any other function, the business will not stay behind to support the weakest link. No CEO will allow his business to be slowed down by non-adapting functions. He will simply bypass them and find outside sources to support the pace and strategy he has charted.

- **Do our users like the information?** This question is tricky. Some IT professionals argue that users do not need to like it. They contend that users should not have a choice in the matter, just as they have no choice over the phone service provided or the facilities hosting their offices. This is a corporate mandate that users need to adhere to. It is exactly this attitude that keeps users away from IT and makes them reluctant to cooperate. In a world where 95 percent of decisions are made subconsciously through emo-tions and not through logic, as per Professor Jerry Zaltman, of the Harvard Business School, and the author of *How Customers Think,* this response might require further examination. Users must like the information if IT professionals expect maximum engagement and not minimal interaction and utilization of information. Users might not like the contention and the message it carries, but they should like the overall product and appreciate the value it delivers to them. Making users like their product depends on better product design, better education, and better communication. Users who like the product cooperate more and make it more profitable for the vendor—in this case, the IT operation. Making users like it is a priority often neglected by IT because of misunderstanding users and the IT role in their function. Ultimately, it is about selling to the users.

- **Do IT professionals promote change in the organization or postpone it?** Ultimately, when the sum of all IT components is calculated, a question about its core role arises. What is the IT role as perceived by its users? Is it a change promoter or change preventer? The answer to this question is critical to understanding the way users relate to IT. As a change promoter, IT might help users achieve their goals and become heroes in their own organizations. As a change preventer, IT is the function that users must avoid if they want to achieve their objectives. The answer to this question determines the complete experience and the type of relationships users have with IT. Will they attempt to increase the IT role or reduce it to the minimum? IT can help determine the direction of that decision.

- **Do IT professionals reinforce business processes or raise them to the next level?** IT must examine its core activities as a subset of the preceding question. It is these core activities that breathe operational life into the core competency. It is what users see and what determines their approach accordingly. If IT spends its resources and time in process reinforcement, it is perceived as a past function, not as a future function. If IT supports change and advances change, it is a future function. IT is part of the company's progress and future, not its dragging legacy.

As product managers and owners, IT should assume full responsibility for the success and acceptance of its products. It can no longer play the role of tool provider. A complete commitment to its product's success is required. Producing it in the spirit of "Build it and they will come" will not work any more. Even in IT projects in which business users are consulted, users often default to their old behavior of using personal Microsoft Excel sheets and Microsoft Word documents and not taking full advantage of new technologies. Millions of dollars of investment are lost because of incompliant users or simple negligence. Old

> " As product managers and owners, IT should assume full responsibility for the success and acceptance of its products. "

behaviors die hard. In the process, it is IT that is blamed for the failure. As product managers, IT professionals must change this track record to change the fate of their projects.

The new prism is required in order to connect IT to its business in terms of accountability and focus on results instead of on facilitating infrastructure. The new prism of information as a consumable product forces IT professionals to reconsider what information they produce, how they deliver it, and to whom. With the purpose of connecting to the core innovation and growth engine of the company, IT must focus on utilization rather than on production. Production creates inventory, and utilization focuses on reducing inventory and ensuring usage that delivers results.

PEOPLE: THE ULTIMATE CHALLENGE

Dealing with information and processes is a relatively easy task (see Figure 2-3). Neither shows much resistance to change and new technology, and both absorb any amount of work conducted by IT. Neither entity shows regrets or demands much from IT professionals. They are passive, nonresistant, and accepting. As such, they are easy targets for the IT operation.

Data collection, compilation, and analysis are simple and clear-cut tasks. Even process uniformity and control are relatively easy tasks. IT can reinforce seamless processes, decrease costs, and create an efficient operation without much resistance.

People, on the other hand, pose a different challenge altogether. Although they stand to benefit the most from information, they seem to be the most resistant to it. Facilitating change, driving business impact, and growing revenues are just some of the benefits people stand to gain from information, although the general notion is that they resist information and tend to minimize its utilization.

Throughout the years, a mutually suspicious relationship has developed between IT and its users. Knowing the perceived limitations of people, IT professionals were attempting to reach their goals with minimal interaction and dependency on their users. IT professionals were counting on their technology expertise to justify their work and hiding behind the technology complexity to keep criticism at bay. Users, for their part, developed a thin skin of resistance to IT projects and technology, assuming that they were meant to restrict their creativity and flexibility in the name of bureaucracy. Users were convinced that they could do just fine without the latest IT technologies, just as they managed to do beforehand.

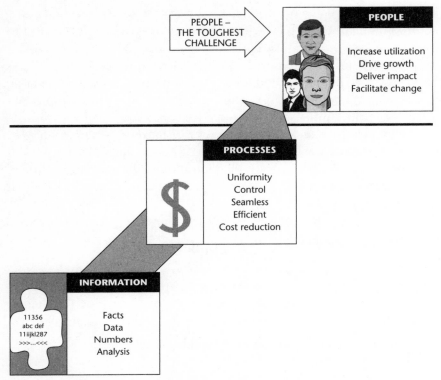

Figure 2-3. People, Processes, Information

But the IT assumption that people are technophobes who develop an immediate resistance to anything new is far from the truth. Just look at the multitude of technologies and software downloaded illegally every day in corporate networks. Lacking training and IT permission, users obtain unauthorized technologies and software that they deem interesting and appealing. They somehow quickly overcome their technophobia and leap into technology expertise. A simple examination of the spread and use of instant messaging (IM) at brokerage houses can portray a clear picture of how dangerous this user behavior can be. Brokers communicate with clients via IM without any of the traditional recording that is applied to their calls and e-mails for the purpose of insurance and security. Brokerage firms are finding themselves exposed to new liabilities in the absence of compliance with corporate guidelines to keep records of all communication with clients. Brokers simply found a technology that they believe is useful and took advantage of it without much resistance or delay.

For generations, people developed mixed feelings about innovation and new technologies. While some people resisted it, others embraced it and took full advantage of it. The difference between those people who rejected new technologies and those who embraced it was not just personal preference and tolerance. It was a vision of usage that was significantly stronger and more appealing than the fear the technology instilled in them.

> " *But the IT assumption that people are technophobes who develop an immediate resistance to anything new is far from the truth.* "

In his book *High Steel,* Jim Rasenberger describes the new technology that evolved in the middle of the 1800s. When steel was introduced, metal-frame construction was invented and enabled the construction of new buildings taller than the existing 10-floor limitation. Until the invention of metal-frame construction, buildings were limited to 10 floors because of the limitation of working with concrete. Metal-frame construction, however, ushered in a new era of skyscrapers, and they started to sprout in major cities in America and Europe. The new technology, however, was welcomed with mixed feelings. On one hand, demonstrations and complaints started. Hidden fears were exposed, supported by physicians and architects who argued that the new tall buildings would spread diseases and turn the streets into a permanent midnight.

In Paris, reaction to the Eiffel Tower was reported by Le Monde in 1901. People believed that the Eiffel Tower would become a huge magnet affecting all nearby houses and would make them permanently tilt toward the new tower.

As a result of public outcry in 1893, the city of Chicago passed an ordinance banning buildings more than 10 stories high. The cities of London and Paris soon followed Chicago's example.

The leaders of New York City, on the other hand, viewed their situation and responded in a completely different way. Viewing the new technology, they saw opportunity and reached the opposite conclusion. They redefined conservative building codes to accelerate the construction of skyscrapers.

It is this single decision that led to New York City's becoming the commercial center it is today. By enabling many companies to consolidate their operations into single buildings, New York's leaders provided a rare incentive for companies to relocate to New York. Chicago, Paris, and London stayed behind too long and lost the race. For decades, they failed to catch up with New York's achievements, despite their subsequent attempts and changes to their original ordinances.

The leaders of Chicago, Paris, and London succumbed to pressure and fears and opted to reiterate the existing and ignore the new. New York's leaders demonstrated incredible foresight and developed a vision of value for the new metal-frame construction technology. It is this vision that allowed them to overcome the public's fears and embrace the unknown, or the new, at the expense of the familiar old.

To overcome the people challenge, IT must take a similar position and develop a vision that inspires its users to cooperate and accept changes. IT must evolve its role from simply implementing and maintaining technology and assume complete responsibility for its users' experience. It is this role that allows IT to connect better with its users and to obtain faster and more complete cooperation and adaptation.

> " To overcome the people challenge, IT must take a similar position and develop a vision that inspires its users to cooperate and accept changes. "

Recently, the faster adoption of several new technologies—such as cellular phones, instant messages, and digital cameras—has taken place. These technologies reached the stage of mass acceptance faster than any other technology before them. These successes indicate that users are willing to go through the learning curve of new technologies. The difference that made these technologies acceptable faster was the concern of their vendors with the total user experience and with a greater commitment to education. By simplifying the experience, enhancing it to deliver an amazing result, and making a commitment to ensure user success and happiness, vendors ensured the accelerated acceptance of these products.

These technologies demonstrate that people's resistance can be conquered, although it requires a people-centric approach and not a technology-centric approach. By focusing on users, IT professionals can design their information to be easy, exciting, and fast to use. Users have no excuse not to take advantage of it.

The people aspect might be a challenging task and difficult to handle, but people are the ticket to IT's renaissance and reconnection to the core of the business. It is user empowerment that drives IT to its innovation role. Without users, the product is just a pile of unused information. With people, the information has better execution and is composed of intelligent decisions. Both are at the core of every growing business.

EMOTIONAL USERS

In considering its customers, IT often views users from the perspective of operators. Users are the people who operate the applications that IT implements. This functional-based view is rather narrow and irrelevant. Users are not just operators. They are indeed far from being automated robots, able to consistently function under any circumstances. In fact, as product managers around the world have already discovered, users are emotional. This fact is not just a matter of how they make their decisions, as just described. It is a matter of how they think, operate, and relate to everything around them.

It is the inability to understand this fact, as well as the lack of willingness to relate to it, that leads many IT professionals to miss their targets because of people issues. For many IT professionals, this matter is irrelevant. They do not see themselves as responsible for the user aspect. As utility operators, they are right. They might as well ignore the aspect of users' emotions. As product owners, they must pay attention to this aspect because it is at the core of their ability to succeed in their task to increase utilization and acceptance.

It is this emotional aspect that makes users embrace or detest new ideas and tools. It is that emotional dimension of users that makes them cooperate and either help IT achieve its new role or make it impossible to achieve. The key is not in users' ability to function and operate technologies and application—it is in their willingness to do so. IT, despite its reluctance, is now more dependent than ever on this emotional aspect.

> " *It is that emotional dimension of users that make them cooperate and either help IT achieve its new role or make it impossible to achieve.* "

3

Redefining Innovation

"The test of a first-rate intelligence is the ability to hold two opposed ideas in the mind at the same time, and still retain the ability to function."

F. Scott Fitzgerald

INNOVATION REDISCOVERED

Innovation is often portrayed as trial and error conducted by a few Einstein–look–alike genius scientists sequestered in their own labs. Using unlimited budgets, these geniuses are the source of all good in their companies. Everyone's eyes look to them for the next new invention that will save everyone from the sea of commoditization surrounding us.

Although some innovation comes from those few select experts, this is not a sustainable model. In the pharmaceutical industry, more than 90 percent of all scientists' efforts result in no breakthrough invention. Most of the research conducted in the labs of Merck, Johnson and Johnson, and Pfizer deliver nothing of significance to these companies. And this result is not for lack of trying. It is simply the nature of the process. The pharmaceutical industry invests many billions of dollars before any blockbuster drug is produced. The companies know very well that the research is, to a large degree, a numbers game. They must invest large sums of money in so many projects in order to come up with few successful drugs. The gamble is high, and so is the reward. But the risk, nevertheless, is significant.

What is innovation—an art or a science? Innovation is defined by *The American Heritage Dictionary of the English Language,* Fourth Edition, as "The act of introducing something new" or "Something newly introduced." Innovation exists everywhere and belongs to everyone, down to the last person in the corporate food chain.

Contrary to popular perception, innovation is not just a matter of creating new products. Apple Corporation invented the PC, the color monitor, the mouse, and the graphical user interface, yet the company owns only 2

> " *Innovation exists everywhere and belongs to everyone, down to the last person in the corporate food chain.* "

percent of the $180 billion global PC market. Dell, on the other hand, which usually joins markets only after they reach some level of maturity, reinvented the business process of direct marketing. This business process allowed the company to surpass Apple by far and achieve more than 30 percent market share in the global PC market. While Apple focused on product innovation, as per the few geniuses in the labs, Dell popularized innovation and empowered all its employees to look into continual improvements to the business model. By doing so, it elevated the innovation process from the rare and the few to everyone. Its dependency on a few select geniuses was reduced dramatically, and it was able to consistently deliver new products to the market and deliver excellent financial results.

INNOVATION BY LUCK OR BY DESIGN

Another common mistake in innovation understanding is the notion that innovation comes whenever it is ready. It is this stroke of lightning that brings those amazing, earth-shattering ideas. People believe that the essence of innovation is an inspiration. This accidental occurrence provides the recipient with a bright new idea not known to the world. But accidents are rare and very difficult to anticipate. You cannot count on the lightning stroke; it comes when it is ready.

This line of thinking is risky. It assumes that the company's fate is dependent on outside forces that behave in an irrational way. This is not a way to run a business. Luck is not a business strategy. Long-term survival and success cannot be based on an arbitrary stroke of lightning. Companies need to plan for innovation just like they plan for success. The two are interwoven. Innovation has to be a product of ongoing, well-defined processes that capture and evaluate innovation regularly and not occasionally. A company should not wait for the innovation to arrive arbitrarily, but, rather, plan for regular, periodical meetings that discuss innovation, the competitive landscape in market trends, new technology availability, and changes in customer preferences and trends in order to create fruitful soil for innovative thinking. By creating innovation by design rather than by luck, companies shift to a more predictable system in which, after establishing it, the risk of arbitrary innovation is eliminated. They take control of the innovation process and lead it rather than be led by it. Innovation by design is about instituting a system, a mechanism that captures and evaluates innovative ideas regularly. It is an integral part of the business operation and is not left to arbitrary availability.

> " *Companies need to plan for innovation just like they plan for success. The two are interwoven.* "

CUSTOMER-DRIVEN INNOVATION

Another popular innovation perception is that innovation comes from listening to customers. Although customers can assist in improving a company's products, their input can hardly be described as innovation. Customers often drive incremental innovation that results in the continuous improvement of products. The business impact caused by those incremental changes is proportionally related to the actual innovation; it is also incremental and cannot be sustained for the long run. If Sony Corporation would have listened to its customers, the Walkman would have never been invented. Twenty-five years after making the courageous decision to not listen to its customers, Sony turned this small device into a huge growth engine with more than 300 million Walkmans manufactured to date. Is this an argument to stop listening to customers? No, it is not. Innovation has two key elements: the Now and the Wow. Companies must manage both elements and retain a delicate balance between them. Focusing too much on the Wow leaves the door open for competitors to refine their raw innovations and steal the market. Focusing on the Now and incrementally moving current products forward distracts their attention from the need for the next big thing that will have an impact on their business beyond 10 percent growth. As argued by Christian Clayton in his book *The Innovator's Dilemma,* it is

> **" If Sony Corporation would have listened to its customers, the Walkman would have never been invented. "**

exactly that success and focus on customers that can result in missing major market trends and business opportunities.

So, although customers are important for incremental innovation, order-of-magnitude innovation largely relies on a company's own initiative. Companies can not and should not wait for their customers to tell them what to do. Their innovation responsibility is much greater. This innovation will come from the collected information and accumulated experience of the company as well as from its users, who are participants in the creation of information and experience. The need for information-based innovation becomes more crucial and requires greater attention to the management of information in the innovation process.

The following sections explore some guidelines that can be of assistance in achieving innovation that is not dependent on a few geniuses, but that is more stable in its flow of ideas. These guidelines will also leverage information to achieve the maximum valid pool of ideas and innovative products and processes.

INNOVATION AS A FAD

In many organizations, innovation is a matter of fad. Company representatives would not admit to it publicly, but their actions speak louder than words. Subject to a boom-to-bust cycle, innovation becomes a matter of choice. When funds are available and the market is doing well, innovation becomes the focus *du jour* in an organization. When the market demonstrates signs of weakness, budgets are slashed and innovation is minimized or shut down. Innovation then becomes incremental and lacks any great potential to lift businesses out of the market weakness. Economic difficulties then become a self-fulfilling prophecy.

Successful, innovative companies treat their innovation not as a fad but, rather, as a strategic asset. They create a systematic, sustainable innovation mechanism that feeds and manages innovation regularly during good times and bad times, and they shift from an unpredictable innovation cycle to a predictable innovation flow that strengthens the company and creates a competitive advantage, especially during tough times. The companies who see their innovation as more than a fad and support it consistently enjoy the benefit of creating significant competitive advantages, especially in tough times, when their competitors are busy stripping themselves from any innovation or new growth opportunities.

INNOVATION SOURCES

Innovation is often misunderstood to be just the creation of a brand-new product. This type of innovation is relatively easy to contain and manage because it is limited to employees in certain departments, such as research and development. It is these people and what they do that dictate changes in a company's innovation process. This flawed assumption leads to the wasting of many other innovative ideas growing within the company and the lack of any nurturing or support. As such, these ideas die without delivering any commercial effect.

> " Innovation is often misunderstood to be just the creation of a brand-new product. "

In reality, innovation encompasses a wide variety of aspects of doing business. Innovation happens across a business. Every employee encounters an innovative idea as he or she conducts business and interacts with people. The innovation sources can be in these areas:

- New products
- Additional services
- Pre-sales services
- New channels for sales
- New support programs

- Additional cross-sales services
- Additional post-sales activities
- Inventory management
- Warehousing
- Billing processes
- Marketing campaigns
- Product shipping
- Forms of products
- Product transformation to services
- New pricing models
- New ways to deliver the products and services
- People training and compensation
- Customization of services
- Cooperation to create differentiated or personalized products
- Design process redefinition

All these are only a fraction of the business aspects where innovation can take place. By definition, it includes a larger number of users who are not contained in the R&D department. They are everywhere, internally and externally, in an organization. Capturing and leveraging their ideas and insight is the challenge of every organization.

When Netflix mounted an assault on the video-rental business, it did not do so by inventing a new product. It simply redesigned a business process. Utilizing similar sources as those just mentioned, it redesigned the pricing and distribution model. Netflix allows its customers to rent as many DVDs or videos as they want for a single price of $19.95 per month. Customers do not need to worry about late fees or renting too many videos per month. The company ships all its DVDs via mail, saving the high costs of real estate traditionally associated with a business, and provide a self-addressed, stamped envelope for customers to send back their videos. Elimination of the real estate and monthly fees are information-based innovation. They allowed Netflix to gain a devoted following and the flattering copying efforts of much larger competitors. Following the information-based guidelines, the company added distribution warehouses, where its customer base grew to allow faster overnight service to enable customers to rent a larger number of movies per month. Utilizing the information as a resource for innovation is a matter of choice. The information is there—the question is what will be done with it.

INNOVATION GUIDELINES

As a follow-up to the discussion about the essence of innovation and its diverse sources, this section discusses some of the most successfully implemented guidelines to maximize the innovation process. Based on the experience of multiple companies in different industries, these guidelines were compiled to provide a more practical approach to implementing an innovation process across the whole organization:

- **Innovation goes beyond the known and expected.** You must leverage the known and predictable and generate new thinking. Repeating the past is following someone else's agenda. Creating something new is about charting a new path for your organization to lead rather than follow. Look beyond the known and expected. It is exactly the use of information to reiterate the existing that gets companies further away from innovation.
- **Make sure that everyone is involved.** Every employee who works for you and observes your way of doing business will have ideas for improvement and innovation. The question is what is done with those ideas. The answer is highly dependent on the environment for innovation and creativity that you nurture in the business. If the tools and incentive exist, employees participate and share their thoughts. Otherwise, they keep them a secret or, even worse, take them outside the company and either provide them to the competition or become competitors themselves.

> " Repeating the past is following someone else's agenda. Creating something new is about charting a new path for your organization to lead rather than follow. "

- **Have an openness to the new and unknown.** Nurturing innovation is about creating an environment that does not dismiss new ideas. This is not as easy to create as it sounds. Plagued by cynicism and conformity, organizational DNA is often resistant to change and the new. Combined with internal politics, this resistance can be a great anti-innovation formula that keeps the organization away from growth. Nurturing innovation requires an environment that first fights those negative phenomena and then creates greater incentives, tools, and awareness to overcome the possible internal negative drivers. Building examples of an organization's experience in embracing the new and unknown and the positive business impact it had should be used to reinforce the desired behavior.
- **Give permission to err.** If mistakes result in dismissal or penalty, no new, risky ideas emerge. Employees turn to consensus and confirmation rather than challenge the status quo. In reality, and despite their willingness

to accept the fact, all executive makes mistakes. Mistakes are part of doing business. One cannot avoid them. It is the attitude toward them that dictates the number of mistakes that are made and the total number of new ideas that are generated. Try celebrating mistakes and rewarding them. Leap to the other side of the spectrum, and you might awaken the best in your employees.

- **Build opportunities to innovate.** Employees who believe that they have discovered something of significance might not be inclined to share it with their employers. A mechanism in which an employee shares the rewards associated with the business impact of their idea can generate greater interest in providing ideas and innovation for the benefit of the whole organization. In numerous cases, technology companies dismissed their employees' ideas only to see them leave and start their own businesses, which then became successful. Some of those technology companies ended up paying many millions of dollars to buy those same companies that delivered the technologies they originally rejected.

- **Diversity is the key to maximizing innovation.** Ideas and innovation often come from the friction that diversity creates. Different viewpoints, based on the different backgrounds of employees, can create a more colorful fabric of innovation than a homogenous organization can create. Facilitate the innovation process with a diverse group of people with different geographical, social, and ethnic backgrounds. Each participant can then apply her own prism and set of criteria to the issue at hand and can contribute a unique insight to create a more complete innovative solution. The more diverse the process, the better the total results.

> " Different viewpoints, based on the different backgrounds of employees, can create a more colorful fabric of innovation than a homogenous organization can create. "

- **Patience is the key to innovation birth.** Patient money is a concept that is often used at 3M, a company known for its ability to consistently churn out innovation. You might not know what will come next from 3M, as is always the case with innovation, but you can count on the fact that something new will come out. If innovation were a matter of quick results, everyone would have done it. But innovation takes time. Real innovation and new ideas take time to mature and become commercially ready. Set them free before their maturity stage, and you will miss the market and the opportunity. Set them free too late, and you might miss the first-mover advantage, although you would still have a market to

sell to and a product worth buying. Subjecting innovation to your quar-
terly results, which means being impatient, will most likely result in small
incremental innovation, but not "the next big thing" that can become
your next money maker. Even though patience is rather scarce these days,
patience pays higher dividends and is therefore worth the wait.

- **Chaos is part of the process.** In a world where everyone tries to fit
  everything into a box and manage it to death, chaos is the anti-corporate
  factor. It is the one factor that ought to be squashed as soon as possible
  and eliminated from the corporate culture. It seems that chaos causes a
  lack of compliance with traditional corporate reports and pie charts; it is
  an undesirable guest in corporate suites. However, it is exactly this lack of
  order that breeds new ideas. If corporations follow their orderly manner,
  they are far less likely to come up with anything new. How could they, if
  they focus all their efforts on reiterating the known and predictable?
  Chaos should be embraced and not ignored or eliminated. Chaos is the
  fruitful soil of innovation. It is where trial and error exists. It is the land
  where seeds of the new grow naturally, unlike the traditional corporate
  world, which rejects them. Chaos should not be created for the sake of
  chaos. This is not a nonprofit exercise of an academic thought. It has to
  have commercial guidelines and outlets for execution. You can read more
  about them in the next section.

- **Collaboration is important to maximizing impact.** Innovation is
  the fruit of many people's work. Even if someone fails to come up with
  the initial thought, that person is crucial to the formation of the idea and
  bringing it to the world in a successful and profitable manner. Therefore,
  collaboration plays an important role in the overall innovation process.
  Unlike the popular perception in which a few geniuses dictate the future
  of innovation, the masses must be engaged to allow enrichment and
  empowerment of the innovation. No company can allow itself to be too
  dependent on a few select people. This situation breeds prima donna
  behavior and results in higher risk for the company's existence. Just like
  the dependency on a few select rainmaker salespeople, which is not a
  strategy for the long run, dependency on a few geniuses is risky and
  unwelcome. Involving as many employees as possible reduces the risk and
  maximizes the impact.

- **Without a process for prioritization, innovation never sees the
  light of day.** "I never saw an idea I did not like." I heard this line from
  one of my clients. It was a frightening thought. Consider working for
  someone who cannot prioritize and apply some logic to the idea process.
  Without prioritization, ideas never make it. They simply start the process
  and then fade out as new ideas are pursued. There is such a thing as too
  much innovation. Too many ideas stifle the process and turn them all into
  irrelevant ideas without an outlet for execution. A common mistake is failing to develop a prioritization system, which is often caused by a lack of
  knowledge or fear of missing out on something. This mistake often results

in losing more ideas and innovation. Often, ideas are pursued just because they were pursued by the right people in the organization. Seniority and titles or fear of standing up to the boss are not logical prioritization systems, but are often used as a default system in the absence of a better one. Such systems ultimately stifle innovation and crush it. A good prioritization system should include guidelines for the evaluation and methods of financially quantifying the proposed innovation. These objective methods should dictate the corporate investment agenda.

- **Innovation is invention meets commercialization.** When invention does not meet commercialization, it becomes art. It might be lovely art, but not in a form that justifies corporate investment. To justify corporate investment, an invention must comply with commercial requirements, among them the requirement to be ready for sale to a large number of customers in order to repay the investment. Often, innovative companies fail in this step. They might encourage inventions and trials and embrace a mistake-acceptance policy, but they fail to cash in on the invention. Their system is not built with a well-defined and executable plan to take an invention to market. As such, they always stay in the experimentation stage and leave the big reward to those who truly learned the power

> " When invention does not meet commercialization, it becomes art. It might be lovely art, but not in a form that justifies corporate investment. "

of business innovation. Although Henry Ford was not the inventor of cars, he nevertheless created one of the most powerful car companies in the world. Unlike other artist-like inventors in the industry, Ford focused his efforts on the commercialization aspect as he invented the way to bring cars to millions. His manufacturing process was a commercialization innovation that brought the original invention to the masses. This is the essence of innovation in a commercial context. Without the commercialization aspect, no company can justify any innovation investment.

OPEN INNOVATION VERSUS CLOSED INNOVATION

Closed innovation is practiced today by many companies. They treat the innovation process as intellectual property to be shared with others only after the exchange of funds. Using this line of thinking, innovation can and must be created internally with no exposure to the outside world. Exposure means the risk of losing the innovation to others. Sharing is translated into minimizing the opportunity and loss of control. This modus operandi characterizes the way organizations approach innovation: Even if they are exposed to new ideas, they often rush to bring them into the internal fold and avoid exposing them to the outside world at any cost.

> " *This modus operandi characterizes the way organizations approach innovation: Even if they are exposed to new ideas, they often rush to bring them into the internal fold and avoid exposing them to the outside world at any cost.* "

This not-invented-here syndrome, which leads many engineers to believe that they can do anything faster, better, and more cost effectively than anyone else in the world has cost many companies much in missed opportunities. Reluctance to cooperate, combined with the attitude "We know better, and no one can teach us anything new" dominated traditional leading R&D facilities from GE to AT&T Bell Labs. This attitude is nothing more than an ego trip. It is not founded in real fact. It is not out of respect and humility that "others might have thought of something we did not." Companies cannot afford this ego-based behavior, which costs them much in missed opportunities, delays to market introduction, and losses in market share.

At a time when innovation is subject to time and competitive pressure, companies no longer have the luxury of practicing closed innovation. Pressured to deliver innovation on an ongoing basis, companies must produce a continuous flow of ideas and inventions. They ought to be able to look beyond their restrictions and limitations and cooperate with as many possible partners to build the largest possible pool of ideas and ways to change their businesses. Those partners range from suppliers and customers to competitors and start-ups. All need to be incorporated into the process and allowed into the inner sanctum of an organization's innovation. This inclusion should not compromise the confidentiality and proprietary aspect of the innovation—these aspects should be guarded. But the guarding cannot and should not come at the expense of greater, open collaboration.

The collaboration in open innovation ranges from the simple validation of ideas to providing brand-new ideas. Open innovation collaborators share insight and information geared toward maximizing the innovation potential and fine-tuning it to be ready for the market introduction, to increase its chances of success. In some cases, open collaboration leads to the lowering of costs and risk as collaborators decide to share their introduction expenses and launch the new idea together. Such collaboration is evolving among competitors. The auto industry, notorious for its high R&D costs, has adopted such cooperation models to reduce its risks and introduction costs.

Open innovation is a must in today's short lifespan of innovations. It enables a greater number of ideas to materialize and increases their chances of success. Just as teams can achieve more than individuals, such is the case with innovation collaboration. More open innovation collaborators can usher in more successful inventions.

DISCIPLINE AND MANAGEMENT

One of Apple's failures in cashing in on its own innovation is the Newton story. The first personal data assistant (PDA) was launched in the early 1990s to a great deal of fanfare by the then-CEO of Apple, John Scully. The product died a slow and painful death following investment in advertising and retail stores. Apple now does not own a single piece of the $3.3 billion market for PDAs. This is another missed opportunity of the company. Apple, as a company, focuses on innovative products. But it fails consistently in taking them to market.

The two critical information-based innovation dimensions are innovation discipline and innovation management. Both dimensions are highly dependent on information to make sense of the chaotic innovation process. By taking advantage of existing internal information, established companies can provide better discipline to the prioritization-and-decision process, to determine which invention or idea will become a commercial product and which idea will stay on the drawing board. It is exactly the same large pool of corporate data, generated through major investment and used to provide an insightful view into the current state of the business, that can be used to evaluate and decide which new ideas justify the investment. Customer purchasing patterns and preferences are among the information that can assist in the decision process and provide a competitive edge over start-up companies, with their heavy reliance on gut feelings and intuition. Utilizing this information during the process reduces the risk dramatically and allows execution with confidence.

Following innovation analysis and selection, innovation management becomes critical. This is where Apple has failed in the past. Busy with the next great idea, Apple failed to develop a channel to maximize the commercial impact of its innovation. The company counted on customers to see the beauty of their innovation and buy it on their own. Communication and market reach, channel management, and customer education were left to luck. But successful innovative companies cannot count on luck. Luck is what the customer might perceive, but companies know better. Luck is the result of many years of effort, a well-planned strategy, and a well-executed plan. Luck has nothing to do with it. Hard work, smart planning, and execution are the cornerstones of innovation management. A lack of innovation management is the reason that first-time innovators often lose their innovation to latecomers who focus on innovating their execution plans. As with innovation discipline, innovation management coupled with information provides a significant edge to established companies over their start-up competitors, who lack all that information. By following past performance indicators, companies know who will be most receptive to their new products and what are the best ways to communicate and educate them to achieve acceptance. Start-up companies, who lack this body of information and past-performance indicators, have to guess and therefore assume a greater risk during the process. A wrong decision might cost them their very existence.

> ❝ Luck is what the customer might perceive, but companies know better. Luck is the result of many years of effort, a well-planned strategy, and a well-executed plan. ❞

Innovation, contrary to popular perception, exists everywhere in an organization. Organizations that fail to understand that fact focus on a few geniuses to save their businesses. This risky strategy has no foundation in real experience. Innovation is not a matter of luck, but, rather, of design. By utilizing information, companies can thrive and take advantage of their accumulated experience to build a powerful innovation machine with clear innovation discipline mechanisms and an execution system, in the form of innovation management, that does not leave them exposed to latecomers who steal their thunder and their hard-earned profits. The first step is dropping old notions and perceptions and realizing that innovation happens everywhere. It is up to these companies to do something about it.

4

The User-Centric Organization

"Knowledge speaks, but wisdom listens."

Jimi Hendrix

PEOPLE: THE ULTIMATE PARTNERS IN SUCCESS

To transform an organization into an innovation-based operation, a major shift has to take place. Information has to play an important role in the organization, in the form of both knowledge and a trigger for new thinking. IT organizations, as part of rethinking their role, have to transform themselves from the traditional production-focused function and become utilization-focused. If IT professionals recognize that people are crucial to the success of both IT and innovation, IT has to go through a transformation and focus on the individual rather than on product information. This shift will not be easy for IT, but it is inevitable.

According to the Strategos consulting firm's 2003 Innovation Survey of 557 executives:

- Fifty-five percent of respondents stated that innovation is more important than it was three years ago.
- Fifty-seven percent of respondents stated that innovation will be more important three years from now.

Respondents claimed that the least effective innovation is implementing a business model. The most common obstacles in the innovation cycle were

- Innovation
- Prioritization
- Innovation
- Realization
- Innovation
- Deployment

A closer examination can demonstrate that these obstacles are all information dependent. All these obstacles can be easily addressed with the right information at the right time and in the right context. In the absence of such information, users are driven to inaction or uncalculated risk decisions. Either option is bound to cost the organization dearly. Without IT and its product—information—these obstacles cannot be addressed and overcome.

> " If IT professionals recognize that people are crucial to the success of both IT and innovation, IT has to go through a transformation and focus on the individual rather than on product information. "

In the same Strategos survey, respondents stated that the top barriers to effective innovation are

- Short-term focus (63 percent of respondents)
- Lack of time and resources (52 percent)
- Lack of systematic process (33 percent)
- Unrealistic payoff expectations (31 percent)

At least three of these four barriers can be addressed effectively by information. The amount of time required in order to assess and implement innovative ideas can be reduced with relevant information that is readily available. The availability of a systematic innovation platform can reduce the amount of required resources and allow proper management of the variety of ideas. An expectation can be realistically set, and therefore achieved, through proper information-based planning. The role of information and IT has never been as important as in the innovation cycle. Users are highly dependent on both elements.

In a Gartner study of the challenges for change in the organization, 56 percent of respondents selected corporate culture as the key barrier to change. The second most important factor in the study was, surprisingly, that 42.4 percent of respondents claimed unyielding IT systems as a barrier to change. IT cannot afford to be the obstacle to change and innovation. Especially during periods when innovation is becoming increasingly more important to the company's success and organizations seek innovation as a survival method, IT must evolve to become more agile and responsive. This transformation starts by focusing on individuals and their needs as opposed to the product. It is no longer acceptable to produce the product first and then search for users. It is time to design the information experience completely from the perspective of the user.

The user experience includes a variety of questions, such as:

- Who are the users?
- What makes them different from each other?
- How do they consume the information?
- What information does each user really need?
- Why should users use the information? What are its selling factors?
- What tools do users need in order to best utilize the information and enhance their total experience?

The transformation of IT to a user-centric and experience-based model involves taking complete ownership of all information utilization. This process requires IT to go far beyond production of the product and into the dissemination and education of users, tasks that are foreign to a production-oriented operation. But, in a world where the management of storage, security devices, and servers no longer defines excellence and can be easily and cost

> " The transformation of IT to a user-centric and experience-based model involves taking complete ownership of all information utilization. "

effectively done outside the company, IT must evolve and learn these new skills. In an era in which innovation plays an increasingly important role in the company's success, IT must adapt to the new agenda and change accordingly, to connect to the core of the business. It is not a matter of choice or degree. It is necessary for survival. It is also a promise for thriving.

USER SEGMENTATION: AUTOMATING THE MASSES VERSUS MAKING A BUSINESS IMPACT THROUGH THE RIGHT PEOPLE

When IT professionals engage in user segmentation, the difference between their current modus operandi and the future becomes clear. User segmentation allows IT professionals to differentiate between users based on their business impact, information consumption, and lifestyles. These new prisms make the current mass service of information irrelevant. The mass production model in which all users are treated in the same way will clearly become financially unjustified.

Looking at the prism of information as a product, the first challenge of IT executives is to ask themselves who the customers are and how they differ from one another. In an information-production approach, IT provides the same information to the masses with little differentiation between individuals. All information is created equal. Some aspects of roles and privileges protect confidential information from the wrong pairs of eyes, but nothing more in terms of a customer-centric approach. In this mass-production model, technology is the core and users adapt to it. It is a user's role to search for the information that's needed and use it at her own risk. As a result, projects often focus on saving two minutes of time for the lowest-paying employees in the organization rather than on assisting the organization's business builders in having the maximum impact on their multi-million-dollar decisions.

In a user-centric model, IT recognizes that not all users are created equal. They are not equal in the amount of information they need, the way they consume the information, or the lenses they use to digest it. Their lifestyles, time sensitivities, and impact on the business create another dimension of differentiation. All these dimensions require creating the information around their business impact and lifestyles to ensure maximum utilization. Users become the center point, and the technology becomes secondary. Users do not adapt to the technology; information adapts to users. Just like good product managers, they must adapt their product to the total customer experience. A user-centric model provides different services to different users. To achieve that, IT first identifies who its different users are and what makes them different so that unique services can be created for each one. The user-centric model maximizes business value and impact. It designs the information in accordance with the requirements of the user and the business, not in accordance with the processes and technology capabilities.

> " *Users do not adapt to the technology; information adapts to users. Just like good product managers, they must adapt their product to the total customer experience.* "

A user segmentation exercise must be conducted in order to identify different users and their different lifestyles and business impact. By conducting this exercise, IT sets priorities of service that are not based on the current crisis mode ("the noisiest users get the attention") but, rather, on more business-driven factors. Usually, the "noisiest" user is the one who has time to make a great deal of noise and is not a major business builder. Rather, he is a low-impact employee. In our experience, the segments described in the following sections should be consistent with most organizations' users (see Figure 4-1).

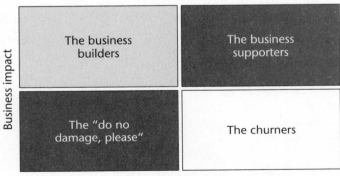

Figure 4-1. User Segmentation

Business Builders

Business builders have a great deal of impact on a company's revenues and costs. These individuals' decisions seriously affect the company's results, and, therefore, their decisions carry a significant level of risk. Business builders should be the first priority of every piece of information and should be prioritized as such in every service provided by IT. Business builders are not just people with seniority or titles. Sales and marketing people, who might not carry high rankings or have a large organization reporting to them, might still be involved in high-risk decisions and deals. As such, it is the business impact criteria, rather than the ranking, that should be applied to categorize the business builders.

Business Supporters

Business supporters are individuals who are enablers of the business builders, and, as such, they have an indirect high impact on a company's revenues and costs. Their sole purpose in the company is to allow the business builders to be effective. Business supporters are high consumers of information. Because their information needs support the decisions made by the business builders, they should be prioritized as such for all information-related services.

Churners

Churners are high consumers of information with a relatively low impact on the business. Churners are the reason that IT cannot deliver better service to those who affect the business. The high degree of noise created by churners because of their high volume of consumption skews IT resources to focus on their crises and requirements. It diverts resources from the business builders and business supporters. IT should carefully assess churners' relative business impact and consumption of IT resources. Churners are likely to consume a disproportionate amount of resources and obtain higher priority than they justifiably deserve.

Do No Damage

Do-no-damage users have low information usage and a low impact on business performance. These users are people whose interaction with information is inconsistent. Their information usage learning curve is high, and they too consume resources and priority because of their lack of practice and usage of the information. Their relatively low usage of information still carries a higher cost of service because of their lack of knowledge of how to consume it. Again, IT professionals find themselves in a position where their services are skewed toward low-impact users because of their lack of expertise in information consumption.

Although it is important to service all users and help them in their information consumption, resource restrictions and a sense of urgency require a different approach. A one-size-fits-all dispensation of services often causes resources to be diverted to churners and do-no-damage users. These resources should be prioritized first for business builders and then for business supporters.

By not segmenting their products and usage and by treating all employees equally, IT professionals end up automating the transactions of secretaries who make $25,000 per year rather than enabling the decisions of executives who make $250,000 per year and have millions of dollars at stake. The user-centric model creates a disciplined method in which information and services are created and distributed. This model helps IT align itself with the business agenda and strategy and not be subject to a continual "firefighting" mode, which is common in many organizations. By focusing on the right users, IT is taking the first step toward switching from a production mindset to a utilization mindset (see Figure 4-2). This focus creates a critical building block toward strategy and execution alignment. User segmentation aligns the IT agenda and resources with those of the executive team and the organization's overall agenda. This is the first building block toward business impact.

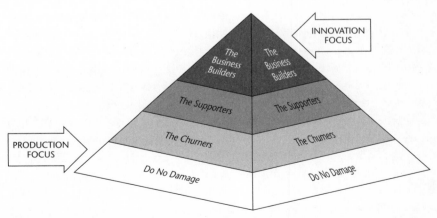

Figure 4-2. User Segmentation Impact

By understanding lifestyle patterns, IT can add another dimension of service differentiation. It is highly likely that many business builders spend a significant amount of their time, more than 50 percent, outside their offices with customers and suppliers. As such, their main view of information is through their PDAs. PDAs do not lend themselves to full information interaction. For these business builders, IT should consider delivering services by exception.

> " *Their focus is to eliminate detailed information and to deal with exceptions.* "

The information should be Blackberry ready and with a quick response incorporated into the designed service. Business builders might not concern themselves with full-length reports. Their focus is to eliminate detailed information and to deal with exceptions. That is how service should be delivered to them.

Business supporters, on the other hand, require a great deal of collaboration and information to support their business builder projects. Access to significant amounts of information, the ability to normalize and prioritize information, and collaboration tools are crucial to their success. They read long reports and dive into detailed information. That is how they get the insight that they then deliver to the business builders. Mobility and exceptions do not play a major role with the business builder supporter who needs to consume large amounts of information. Their lifestyles do not require it, either. Details and information availability, combined with business intelligence, are their top priority.

By nature, churners do not travel. Instead, they stick to a single office location. Self service is more suitable to them. Although IT might complement business builders with phone-based support, churners should be exclusively directed to Web-based support. Their timeframes and sense of urgency are different from those of business builders. This fact, combined with their business impact, does not merit a high-maintenance program. Because they're primarily office based, they clearly do not justify the high-touch service offered to business builders. Churners do not live by the same time pressures, they do not deal with the same budgets or sales quotas, and they do not work remotely.

Many do-no-damage people might not have access to dedicated computers. They might be manufacturing workers or warehouse clerks, for example. For them, especially with their low usage, which comes with high support costs because of a lack of expertise, electronic kiosks might be the solution. All these users' key interactions and queries should be placed in an easy-to-use dedicated kiosk that reduces the cost of service and maintenance by simplifying processes and interactions.

Avoiding the trap of automating the tasks of an employee who makes $25,000 a year at the expense of information needed to make decisions with millions of dollars in impact is the direct result of customer segmentation and understanding that not all users are created equal. In customer segmentation, IT does not refer to the occasional call from the executive assistant of the CFO demanding the repair his Blackberry. This is an exception, not the rule. A new rule should be instituted in which users are defined and prioritized and are provided with service. An occasional call from the CFO covers crisis management and firefighting mode. This mode is exactly the same as the one that got IT into trouble. User segmentation focuses on building a method to prioritize and service different users differently.

User segmentation is all about business consideration rather than about ego or prestige. Segmentation is not about executive privileges. As discussed earlier, some non-executives might be qualified for some high-touch services, based on their roles and responsibilities. This segmentation focuses on alignment. Aligning resources with users is an alignment between the way users operate and consume information against their business impact, the information they need, and the way they need it to get the job done effectively.

5

Redesigning the Decision Process: Leveraging Information to Ensure Business Impact

"Our knowledge is a little island in a great ocean of non-knowledge."

Isaac Bashevis Singer

USER EXPERIENCE INFORMATION

Following customer segmentation, the next step in building a user-centric business model is adapting to the user's experience. Decisions are at the heart of a user's experience with information. Decisions are, by nature, about assuming risk and steering the organizational ship to new and unknown, yet promising, horizons. Although decisions differ by degree of risk and impact, they are nevertheless at the heart of any organization's life. Without decisions, there is no execution. Inaction is placing you on a fast pace to market irrelevance and elimination. As crucial as decisions are to every organization's future, they are the fear of many users and the hubris of others. Some users try to delay making decisions because of the potential negative consequences of making the wrong one. Other users make decisions so quickly that they are made without serious consideration and evaluation. Overconfident, these users assume greater risk than they should and place the whole company on a risky path.

> ❝ *Inaction is placing you on a fast pace to market irrelevance and elimination.* ❞

Decisions, whether delayed or irresponsible, are at the heart of an organization's user experience. Users often regard participation in decision-making processes as a sign of importance in the organization. Not being part of certain decisions is, equally, a sign of diminishing importance. "I decide; therefore, I exist" is the mantra of many users.

Improving and connecting to these users' experiences is an opportunity for IT, as part of its transformation, to look at information from the user perspective. Providing and redesigning information to support decisions and adapting it to the way users need it in order to make decisions is the challenge at hand. Because decisions today are made with little supportive information, IT must bring information to a new level that creates support and execution mechanisms for decision makers. Even if users continue to make intuitive decisions, there is room for information to enhance the quality of the decisions and to direct the execution of these decisions. The role of information will shift to the following areas:

- Identify and manage risk.
- Fine-tune decisions.
- Provide execution guidance.
- Change management.
- Analyze what-if? and why-not? scenarios.

In her book *The March of Folly,* the American historian Barbara Tuchman examines the tendency of governments and leaders to act stubbornly and often against logic and their countries' best interests. This tendency is what Tuchman characterizes as folly. Her study analyzed the way leaders make decisions and utilize available information. To qualify as a "folly" decision, the following criteria must be met:

1. First, an opposite alternative was seen by the leader's contemporaries.
2. Second, a better option for actions was available at the time of decision.
3. Last, the mistaken (folly) course of action was followed by a group rather than by an individual.

These criteria enabled the researcher to distinguish between an insane tyrant's decision and a true folly decision. In her book, Tuchman cites a multitude of examples, ranging from the Trojans' fateful decision to allow the Trojan horse into their city to the loss of the British colonies in America to the failure of U.S. policy and actions during the Vietnam War. All the cases listed demonstrate that people's utilization of relevant, available information is less than desirable even if the stakes are high and the ultimate impact can be determined. Leaders have repeatedly selected to ignore available information and act on a different, non-information-based set of considerations. In all these cases, ignoring information led to fatal consequences.

Humans have a spotty track record of making decisions by the utilization of available and relevant information. Drawing on the study in *The March of Folly,* I would argue that despite the greater availability of larger sets of information and knowledge, people do not take advantage of it to better their decisions and performance. On its own, information (and its abundant availability) does not produce consistently better executive decisions. Unless information is sold to users and delivered in a certain way to them, it will not, despite its significant value, positively affect decisions and execution. Users must take advantage of information. They need to want to do so, to make it useful. IT produces information with the mentality "Build it and they will come." In reality, information utilization in organizations is less than desirable. Clients often use

> " *Humans have a spotty track record of making decisions by the utilization of available and relevant information.* "

terms such as "decision over lunch," "decision at golf," or "decision drinking beer," but rarely do they use the term "decision by information." In his research, Daniel Kahneman, the economics Nobel prize recipient and Princeton professor, reaffirms this trend and discusses the inclination of people to make intuitive, rather than reason-based, decisions. In his work, Kahneman demonstrates that, in groups, people tend to take greater risks and ignore reasoning. They assume that the risk is being shared by the whole group.

"Businesses are not investing in trying to figure out what they've done wrong. That's not an accident. They don't want to know." This statement by Kahneman best illustrates the reluctance to evaluate decisions and to be held accountable. Organizations prefer to continue functioning in the state of intuition they are already in.

To drive innovation and growth in organizations, information must be better utilized to ensure the maximization of opportunities and execution. These studies only reiterate the void existing in organizations today regarding information utilization and the potential for IT professionals to take ownership of this critical void.

DECISION PROCESS REDESIGN

In taking ownership of the decision process, IT might face a challenge created by the intuitive nature of decisions made by human beings, who are often too human to be logical. However, a major role in transforming those decisions into intelligent decisions awaits the information experts (see Figure 5-1):

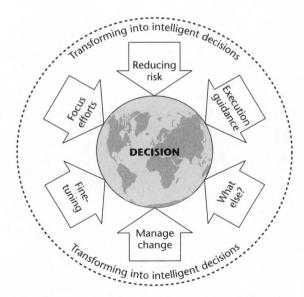

Figure 5-1. Redesigning the Decision Process

- **Reduce risk.** To minimize the risk associated with certain decisions, information plays a major role in evaluating those potential risks and in providing guidance based on the company's history and accumulated knowledge. It also provides available information to ensure that decisions do not bear significant risks and as such are ready for execution. Risk assessment and mitigation are information-based activities that must accompany every major decision.
- **Fine-tune the decision.** Intuitive decisions are often general by their nature. They provide a general direction, but not a clear picture. These decisions carry a certain amount of vague dimension. Transforming them into clear decisions and adding details that the executive making the decision often did not bother with is an information-based challenge. This dimension of the decision is another one in which information should play a role. The company's knowledge should be utilized to ensure a clear, guiding decision that eventually leads to execution. Missing this level of detail and clarity will doom the best decisions because employees will not know what to do with them. Sometimes, employees create personal interpretations that might be off the mark from the original intended decision, or they might ignore the decision altogether because they do not know what it really meant. Information-based fine-tuning can solve this problem and accelerate execution through clarity and the details provided.

> " *Risk assessment and mitigation are information-based activities that must accompany every major decision.* "

- **Focus efforts.** Trade-offs are critical to decision execution. Without them, a decision is just another item in a long to-do list. Without prioritization, a decision lands in the respectable position of last on the list. Focusing efforts involves creating a context in which the decision will be executed. It should provide evaluation and prioritization of the decision in light of other efforts and allow employees to focus their efforts. An additional aspect of focusing efforts is identifying potential obstacles and challenges. Knowing where upcoming problems might be can often save the innovation altogether from unnecessary failure. This knowledge also allows for the faster removal of these obstacles and the avoidance of unnecessary delays or costs. To do so, an information-infused mechanism that measures and evaluates the consequences and available resources should be in place to move the decision on the path to execution.
- **Manage change.** Any new decision represents both a threat and an opportunity. If a decision is not managed well, it is often perceived as a threat more than as an opportunity and, as such, results in negative reaction and, often, inaction. Change management based on information helps

employees see the opportunity and reduce the threat associated with the change-driven decision. By using information to help employees manage change, information supports another dimension of the decision actualization.

> " Any new decision represents both a threat and an opportunity. "

- **Play what-if? scenarios.** An important aspect of making a decision is maximizing its impact and eliminating other options. Playing what-if? scenarios is one method to achieve that goal. By examining other possible ways to solve the same problem, companies obtain a higher degree of resolution-maximizing ideas and enhance their overall decisions. Playing what-if and why-not involves examining multiple alternatives and direct and indirect possibilities to address the issue at stake. This examination requires information to establish the other possible alternatives and to examine, prioritize, eliminate, and ultimately support the final decision. This support might include dimensions from the other alternatives that enhance the original decision and make it more viable and prone to success. Playing what-if? scenarios also supports the change management process because they overcome the traditional objections of other individuals who believe in the other alternatives. After these scenarios are examined and taken into consideration, the decision achieves a higher degree of acceptance and readiness for execution. This aspect of any decision is often neglected as impulsive decisions move from thought to execution at a faster pace then ever.
- **Guide execution.** Providing a context for execution is critical to any decision. Without it, the decision lives in a vacuum and is regarded as irrelevant to the company's operation. Moving from a 50,000-foot general decision to a 500-foot executable action plan is a common challenge. This journey requires information in order to chart its course. A lack of guidance leads to flawed execution, if not an absence of execution. Executives often tend to throw their decisions on lower-ranking managers for execution without any real guidance beyond general direction. Information can provide that level of detailed execution guidance and can transform the decision into a meaningful activity. After information is derived from a company's history, the accumulated information can assist management in directing a decision to the right customer base, whether it is the proper geography, the people best suited to be early adapters, the suppliers who can best deliver cost-effective components, or the most appropriate staff member to execute the decision. Providing execution guidance, therefore, is critical to the success of the decision and its intended impact on the business. A lack of information renders the decision useless, out of context, and risky to execute.

Although the likelihood is slim that IT can completely change the impulsive and intuitive nature of decision making in its organizations, it can move it toward reason-based decision making. By providing information during every aspect of the decision process, IT is bound to assist executives in avoiding unnecessary risk or making wrong decisions altogether. Providing execution guidance and an organizational context will drive the decision toward execution in general and higher-quality execution in particular. IT and information have a growing role to play in the decision process in their organizations. Counting on users to take advantage of self-service-based information is an illusion. Only if IT professionals seize the opportunity and assume a greater role and responsibility for their information product do they have a chance to redesign the decision process and make it more informative—and therefore business-driven and less risky and impulsive.

> " *Counting on users to take advantage of self-service-based information is an illusion.* "

Connecting and influencing the decision process links IT to the heart of a company's business. Decisions are at the heart of the innovation and growth challenges of any organization. It is how executives stir their businesses from the common path to new and promising frontiers. Making the wrong decision can be detrimental to any business. Not executing the right decision is equally detrimental to the fate of an organization. The challenge is awaiting a new owner. The owners of information are best suited to take this challenge.

6

The Holistic View of Information: What Else Is Missing?

"Anyone who stops learning is old, whether at twenty or eighty. Anyone who keeps learning stays young. The greatest thing in life is to keep your mind young."

Henry Ford

TOO MUCH FROM TOO MANY DIRECTIONS

The information overload that users face today makes information utilization less and less appealing. Bombarded by huge amounts of often conflicting information, users choose to ignore everything. They are reaching the point where the variety of information is too much to comprehend. They are abandoning all efforts to decipher the information and turn it into meaningful knowledge. The absence of tools to help make sense of the ever-increasing quantity of information leaves users with little choice in their fast-paced decision-making process. They simply choose not to use it.

Internal information, which is the sole domain of IT work, is not the only piece of information users count on in their decision process. They

often examine and consult outside sources of information, such as
regulatory information, competitive information, new technological
advancements, and market research. These sources tend to exacerbate the
information problem. They add to the amount of information required
to be digested and make it impos-
sible to intelligently evaluate and

> " Bombarded by huge
> amounts of often conflicting
> information, users choose to
> ignore everything. "

draw conclusions. The growing
amount of information pushes
users to ignore it or use it only
for marginal decisions.

Another evolving problem is
that without a process for comparing and assessing the wide
variety of information, it often appears conflicting and therefore confusing. As a result, different users use different information to support
their intuitive positions and proposed decisions. As such, the organization as a whole is driven into inaction and delays because of the inability to make sense of conflicting resources. In this case, information
drives the opposite effect by not only not supporting a decision but also
confusing the process altogether.

If IT assumes responsibility for a user's experience, it assumes ownership of the complete picture of information. IT has to engage and
own the complete set of information resources and provide them to its
users. It is also challenged with developing the tools and methods to
assess and evaluate the different, often conflicting sources of information
in order to help users make sense of it all and transform it into useful
decision-supporting information.

Outside sources of information, such as competitive analysis, product comparisons, customer surveys and feedback, and regulatory
requirements are all part of users' overall information experiences.
Rather than focus just on internal information, IT should assume the
responsibility of helping its users with all their information needs. This
includes two elements:

- The first element is the conventional means of acquiring necessary sources
  of information.
- The second, and more important element, is helping to develop the tools
  to understand and prioritize information so that it becomes meaningful
  and useful.

Disseminating information so that it becomes a useful operational tool requires both education and mentoring to ensure that users are ready to adapt to a new way of doing business. Technology vendors and IT professionals should prepare for the complete ownership of information dissemination and not merely do application training. This new methodology is part and parcel of introducing technology. The new success metrics should include not only successful implementation and integration of systems but also complete user acceptance and usage.

ADDITIONAL SOURCES OF EXTERNAL INFORMATION

The average user is exposed to a wide variety of information during the day. According to some sources, the average person is exposed to between 3,000 and 5,000 advertising messages a day—and that is before they even check the news or examine their e-mail messages. These sources of information are a mix of internal and external information, intended and unintended. IT-produced information provides users with the state of affairs of their businesses and, hopefully, some "trendable" information that can lead to action on the part of users. This internal information is critical to their decision process and is assumed to be accurate and of

> **" According to some sources, the average person is exposed to between 3,000 and 5,000 advertising messages a day— and that is before they even check the news or examine their e-mail messages. "**

high integrity. Users often become dependent on this information and take it for granted. External information ranges from the latest regulatory guidelines, such as HIPAA for health-related companies, to the Sarbanes-Oxley Act, which is applicable to wide, cross-industry organizations. The latest competitive moves are playing an important role as well in users' consideration and frame of reference. New technology discoveries and trends are another source of external information. All these sources of external information surround users everywhere, demand their attention and understanding, and continually challenge their assumptions and decisions.

This external information, which is not IT designed or produced, often throws a curve at users. It confuses them and requires them to analyze and compare the information with their internal set of information to better guide their decisions. The external information often challenges users, who often assume that it is superior to internally produced information. Users tend to allocate a higher degree of importance to external information and prefer it over internal information. Because external information is not in their control, users assign a greater weight to it and assume it to be more valid, relevant, and substantial. This attitude is related to "The neighbor's grass is greener" syndrome, where users always assume that whatever is outside their domain is better.

Intended information is information that users actively seek as required for their decisions. Competitive information is a good example. They can engage in an active search and obtain it from multiple sources. They usually know what they plan to do with the intended information and how it should be used, and as such it fits better into their worlds. The findings are subservient to their assumptions and plans and take better advantage of the intended information.

Unintended information, on the other hand, is information that users stumble on. Reading the latest news, trends, or reports or making a discovery in a web portal that they happen to explore might expose a new piece of information. Reading about a new way of doing business or finding a trend in a remote geographical location or a business story might ignite an idea. Unintended information challenges users and often throws them off course as they attempt to ft the new set of information into their existing world. In attempting to take advantage of the newly discovered idea and information, users struggle with the suitability of the new idea in their existing decision system and strategy roadmap.

Multiple sources of information, especially in today's wider, faster access to information, challenges users. Facing their own human imitations, the more information they are exposed to, the less they take advantage it. The confusing nature of the out-of-context information leads users to simply ignore it.

ASSUMING RESPONSIBILITY FOR COMPLETE INFORMATION

As part of its redesign of its users' experience, IT has to assume a greater role in understanding the sources of information facing its users and assist them in addressing the bigger picture. From a user's perspective, the internally designed and produced information is merely a piece of the complete picture and often is not the most important one. IT, by designing its services to include the external sources of information and streamlining them for users, will make a giant step toward its users' perspective. This leap is not just a courteous gesture, but is intended to increase the utilization and effectiveness of their decisions as well as reduce the business risk. By allowing users to understand and prioritize the various, seemingly conflicting sources of information, IT will transform its users into effective, intelligent decision makers.

Users do not now have a system that assembles and normalizes all their available information. The closest related service is a trade analyst, such as Gartner and Forrester, which analyzes the variety of information out there and draws a conclusion. As effective as its research might be, it is lacking in several ways. Designed to be sold to a mass market, it is usually too generic to be able to draw specific conclusions. Because the company serves conflicting competitors and is under ongoing pressure from a variety of competing vendors, the research has to be balanced to the point that it might not be as useful. The research is often descriptive and risk averse rather than futuristic because the research firm tends to be cautious. Ultimately, research firms do not own the actual decisions and are not privy to internal constraints. As such, users who take advantage of the available research often find themselves back where they started from, with the full responsibility to make their own decisions, suitable for their businesses, based on their own constraints and core competencies.

So, IT professionals still need a system that allows users to assemble, assess, and utilize information, especially when it appears to be conflicting and is often overwhelming. This is where IT comes in. By assuming the responsibility for users' perspective of information, IT will take ownership of the complete picture of information. The complete picture includes but is not limited to the issues described in the following sections.

> **" So, IT professionals still need a system that allows users to assemble, assess, and utilize information, especially when it appears to be conflicting and is often overwhelming. "**

EXTERNAL INFORMATION

External information has the potential to enhance and fine-tune strategies and decisions. But it is often used for the opposite purpose. Lacking any control over external information, users tend to exaggerate its value and, in the process, belittle the value of their own internal information. By doing so, they doubt their decisions and strategies and rush to replace them with generic recommendations driven from the external information. These unmanaged moves are dangerous and might cost an organization its core competency and reason for maintaining customer relationships and loyalty.

> " Lacking any control over external information, users tend to exaggerate its value and, in the process, belittle the value of their own internal information. "

On the other hand, some users experience internal information completely differently. They are inclined to assume that the external information is meant to reinforce their existing intuition. These users never bother to go beyond affirming anecdotal pieces of information they find that support their existing positions. In a sense, they use the external information as a tool to prove their points rather than approach it with an open mind and try to understand what it really means.

Either behavior, the panic-based or the dismissal-based, is damaging to a business. Both attitudes require assistance in terms of building a process that allows users to learn from the external information without unnecessarily risking strategy and decisions. Disseminating external information to the point that it is useful and has an impact is another dimension of the IT role in users' experiences. Throughout their experiences, users deal with these types of external information:

- **Market research.** This source of information, which often comes from multiple sources, such as trade analysts, trade publications, and customized research, suffers a similar fate. Users often do not take full advantage of it or use it to reaffirm their intuition rather than as a driver for innovation and new ideas. Because the information is out of context or too generic, it is sometimes ignored or used only for validation purposes. Market research is a large budget item in many users' budgets, despite the rather partial or incremental impact it delivers.

- **Focus groups.** This form of market research is often qualitative by nature. It samples customers' thoughts and ideas. Focus groups have a certain danger because customers often cannot envision futuristic ideas. If focus groups' recommendations were followed religiously, successful products such as the Sony Walkman or the Chrysler minivan would never have seen the light of day. Rejected by customers in focus groups, these and many other products faced the danger of cancellation. This costly source of information requires a better way to understand and assess its valuable information and place it in the correct context.

- **Analysts' reports.** As mentioned, analysts labor daily to assess and evaluate market trends and directions. They produce reports that describe their opinion and interpretations of the market. The keys to their research are words, interpretations, predictions, and opinions. As objectively as analysts attempt to portray their work, it is still the result of human, non-automated work. Especially when forecasting is involved, an element of faith is included in their reports. Analyst reports often wreak havoc in user assumptions and execution. They might redirect their efforts following the latest report they have read, not realizing that by doing so they follow well-publicized agendas that their competition will probably follow as well. In the end, all competitors end up on par after a great amount of investment and effort. Understating analysts' research and reports in the context of corporate strategy is critical to not falling into the trap of following someone else's agendas or keeping on par with the competition.

- **Performance benchmarks.** Performance benchmarks are playing an increasingly important role in users' decisions and execution. They look to competitors and other vendors to define their agendas and priorities. Users assume that what worked for others should work, even with a bit of adaptation, for them as well. In some sense, it is a lazy policy of not inventing the wheel but, rather, following someone else's inventions. Although users have plenty to learn from the experiences of others, especially in the elimination of possible mistakes, this method should be placed in context. One person's strategy might not suit someone else. The low cost of a provider's operational efficiency should not guide premium provider decisions. Placed in context, performance benchmarks can be very useful. Out of context, they are detrimental to the differentiation strategy.

- **Regulatory information.** As discussed earlier, all government offices and other regulatory entities issue their requirements on a regular basis. Judging from the latest requirements, such as the Sarbanes-Oxley Act (SOA) or HIPAA, these regulatory acts confuse more than they clarify. How to comply with these regulations is anyone's guess. You would be hard pressed to find a single security vendor that does not claim that its application allows IT and organizations to comply with SOA or HIPAA. Users facing these regulatory requirements are often confused about what they really mean to their businesses. What changes will they require? How do the changes need to be implemented? Users need significant assistance to make sense of all this regulatory information and how to effectively execute it.

- **New technologies and advancements.** It might be in the form of a knock on the door or an unsolicited e-mail from the CEO. "What are our plans for the new X technology?" the CEO might ask, expecting an immediate operational plan in response. New technologies and advancements plague users, who are unsure what to do with them. They read about them during the hype period and struggle to make sense of them and incorporate them, with minimal risk, into their strategic plans and product roadmaps. Especially when it comes to technology-oriented advancements, IT plays a crucial role in helping users understand new technologies and brainstorm about what innovation can be created with them. The ability to digitize music existed before a commercial outlet such as the iTunes store was available. Smart IT professionals went ahead and digitized their music, anticipating the natural evolution of a sales outlet. Others waited for the commercial channel to be developed first, but lost out on the opportunity because they would have to then start the digitization process.

COMPETITIVE INFORMATION

Competitive information bears a higher degree of interpretation in a user's decision process and strategy formation. Often taken out of context and assigned greater value, competitive information causes users to abandon perfectly designed strategies and become reactive to the latest competitive move. When users are unready for competitive moves, they often panic and react illogically, by attempting to respond to the competitive move rather than strengthening their own core competency position.

> " *Often taken out of context and assigned greater value, competitive information causes users to abandon perfectly designed strategies and become reactive to the latest competitive move.* "

The nature of competitive information and the difficulty involved in obtaining it gives this information a greater level of urgency. A well-designed process is required in order to respond to competitive information from a position of strength rather than weakness. Users require greater assistance in digesting and responding to competitive information. Competitive information varies and includes different aspects of the competitive landscape. Competitive information may include:

- **Product or service comparison.** This is one of the most difficult elements to obtain. In many industries, competing products or services are not readily available. In most industries, even if they are available, it is illegal to investigate them through mechanisms such as reverse engineering. Users, on the other side, are obsessed with the need for product comparison and sometimes obtain product information through illegal sources. Building a mechanism for information collection, validation, and comparison will be of significant help to users seeking to make sense of all the competing information. Identifying the true and the false in competitors' claims about new products and discerning promised features from those that are truly delivered is critical for users' decisions. Information-based mechanisms can help them make the right decisions.
- **Channel and sales analysis.** A go-to-market strategy is often the way companies win. It is often not the best product that wins, but, rather, the one that is most available through multiple channels and promotions. Understanding channel and sales information is even more difficult because this information is highly guarded at every company. Analyzing available information and understanding the patterns, assumptions, and actions associated with them is of great benefit from to users. Crafting a competing go-to-market strategy is a challenge that can benefit from any assistance that IT-based information can provide.
- **Post-sales service structure.** If channel and sales analysis information is difficult to obtain, post-sales service is truly impossible to obtain. Conducted outside the view of non-customers, this information is not shared unless an unsatisfied customer "spills the beans." Finding legal ways to analyze the few bits of information that are available and to understand and construct this strategy is critical to every user. The post-sales service often contains the core competency and value proposition to customers. As such, it is an important research component that users will attempt to obtain.
- **Overall performance.** Although recent regulatory requirements force companies to deliver greater transparency to their operation, it is still not easy to truly understand the total performance of competitors. In many cases, competitors are private and, as such, are not subject to those requirements. Users often try to construct the overall performance from bits and pieces of information shared by their competitors' executives in different press interviews or through analysts' reports. Collecting those bits of information consistently, building them into useful patterns, and comparing them to internal performance are all important functions in which IT can play an important role.

EMERGING SOURCES

Any new emerging source of information, such as RFID, brings with it a new promise. This promise for new insights can assist in running a business better and more competitively. Many of these new information-based insights are heralded as they move from the abacus days to the future of knowledge. Examined on its own, this will probably be true. Any new insight into a business can assist executives in doing a better management job. But the reality is quite different, already reaching the tipping point, where more information is equal to too much information and executives face an information crisis. Information becomes an unmanageable monster that must be tamed and brought back to a proper, manageable perspective, a manageable perspective that makes it useful.

The challenge of IT in owning the complete picture is to develop tools to transform the new, emerging sources of information from a potential burden into a useful, actionable knowledge.

Users are starting to take advantage of emerging, nontraditional sources of information, in addition to traditional sources. Many of these sources pose a new challenge for IT because they might not be structured in the way IT knows how to consume and analyze them. But this lack of structure should not be deceiving. Their value is nevertheless important and critical—sometimes, more so than the traditional sources.

A shift is taking place from formal relationships and sources with both customers and users, such as vendor–customer and employee–employer, toward informal relationships. Customers depend less and less on vendors as a source of information and validation and collaborate with customers like them who provide the verdict over products and services. Technology facilitates this shift in customer–vendor relationship because it makes it easier to locate "informal experts" who are ready and willing to share their knowledge and opinions.

> " A similar shift is influencing employee–employer relationships: Employees are shifting toward less formal sources of information and ways to conduct business. "

A similar shift is influencing employee–employer relationships: Employees are shifting toward less formal sources of information and ways to conduct business. Rather than count on traditional sources of information to conduct business and make decisions, they now approach informal sources that challenge the traditional business thinking. At best, some of these emerging sources would have been considered anecdotal in the old way of information collection.

Social networks have proven effective in allowing people to find their soulmates and new friends. People are willing to place personal and intimate information on web sites geared toward matching people with similar interests. This type of social network has evolved to the next level of facilitating business cooperation between friends and friends of friends. The traditional influencers of commerce, such as advertising, marketing, and selling, are facing newly found competitors in the form of friends and acquaintances. These networks of friends represent a new source of information and a user-centric method of doing business.

Blogs have also emerged as new, unstructured sources of information. From the early days, when they simply shared personal insight, they now are potentially competitive weapons. Employees post company information, sometimes with the support of their employers. Employers who support these efforts are seeking to portray a friendlier face for their companies and leverage the human aspect of their businesses: their employees.

> " *Blogs have also emerged as new, unstructured sources of information. From the early days, when they simply shared personal insight, they now are potentially competitive weapons.* "

Both blogs and social networks have emerging information that will be a necessary ingredient in a user's future information diet.

Blogs and social networks are new emerging sources of information, in the form of audio and video. This unstructured data, which was clearly ignored until recently by many corporations and users, is evolving as an important data source. These technologies, evolved to allow better analysis and insight extraction. As such, they are more useful and relevant to the decision process.

Customer voices shared and recorded in contact centers or in retail stores are "trendable" and therefore useful. Ideas and suggestions shared by customers should be captured and shared with relevant decision makers, especially during a critical decision process. As customers interact with products, wireless videocameras can capture their behavior to allow product managers to better understand the way the products affect customers. Interactions between customers and products in real-time and in a natural, unobtrusive environment provide by far more relevant and critical decision support information.

Emerging sources of information that are not yet on the IT horizon can add significant value to users and their decisions. It is these informal sources that support a user's informal approach and allow them to make more holistic and complete decisions.

When designing a user-centric model, IT should consider these and other emerging sources of information and bring them to users' attention and decision-making process.

NORMALIZATION: MAKING SENSE OF IT ALL

Beyond the collection and consolidation of information into a platform that allows comparison and access to it in a simple and fast manner, IT has one more important role in information assembly. To transform information into useful knowledge, IT needs to build a process that normalizes and then prioritizes those sources of information. Without such mechanisms, the information remains overwhelming, conflicting, and, therefore not useful.

By creating a process that can be justified if shared by many users, IT transforms the piles of information into useful knowledge. The process needs to take into account the available internal information, external information, and competitive information. With a weighted average system, IT can then make sense of its conflicting messages. Emerging sources of information, such as audio and video recording and analysis as well as blogs and social networks, are a new challenge for IT because some of the information will be unstructured and difficult to catalog. But this difficulty should not deter IT from tackling this

> " By creating a process that can be justified if shared by many users, IT transforms the piles of information into useful knowledge. "

challenge. The hidden value in those sources might surpass the value in the traditional information that is available to all. The emerging sources, if captured and understood well, have the potential to be a true competitive advantage.

The next step is prioritization. By assigning importance based on source credibility, seriousness of information, business impact, and meaning of information, IT can start processing the multiple sources of information and deliver it to users in a meaningful and actionable way. Alerts can then be created for the pieces of information that bear the most danger or opportunity for those requiring immediate response.

Making sense of all the information is even more important than collecting it. Even for emerging sources of information, without the ability to prioritize and weigh the different sources, they have the countereffect of confusing rather than supporting. Companies spend significant amounts of money collecting external information. Focus groups and market research can result in staggering expenditures. Not to use this information after all—or to use it for incremental, less important decisions—is unacceptable. Yet, users, facing the overwhelming amount of information, do not have much choice. More means less for them. From the standpoint of user experience, they would rather have less, although meaningful, information and would rather have actionable information than information that is useless. It is the IT challenge to step into this paradox and help users make sense of the complete picture of information they view from multiple sources and the conflicting messages they receive. Doing this will have a direct impact on the quality of decisions and a company's competitiveness in the marketplace.

7

The New Role of Information

"Computers are boring. They only provide answers."

Pablo Picasso

WHAT QUESTIONS?

This famous expression from Pablo Picasso provides an interesting insight into the world of information. If information is used primarily to reiterate the current way of doing business, its value is limited. However, if IT professionals can learn to use the information to answer new questions, they will again connect the information to the core focus, which is growth.

Information should be used not just to deal with incremental progress and process optimization, but also to generate and illuminate questions such as "What if?" and "Why not?" (see Figure 7-1). This process will allow organizations to explore new growth frontiers through existing ones and to gain new customers with existing and new technologies. The greater the degree of disruption the question causes, the greater the potential for innovation and to affect the business. To achieve this situation, IT professionals must change the way they look at information. They have to stop viewing it in the old boring way and start using it to ask new questions.

70

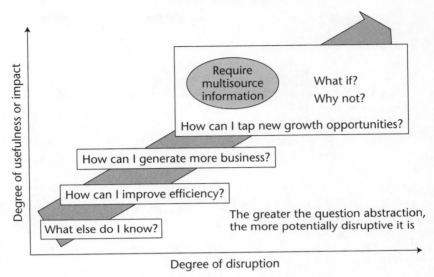

Figure 7-1. How Disruptive Are Your Questions?

Most companies take advantage of their information to reaffirm and reinforce known knowledge. Information is often used to substantiate low-risk decisions, such as how to incrementally increase business with cross-selling efforts. Although this method is effective, it diverts attention from key strategic questions. If information is used as a tool for low-disruption questions, such as "What else do I know?" or "How can I increase efficiency?," it is not used for innovation-based questions that carry the factor 10X possible changes. The questions of "What if?" and "Why not?" create scenarios that can assist a company in discovering a new way of doing business or a new way of manufacturing, or even brand-new products and services.

> **"Information is often used to substantiate low-risk decisions, such as how to incrementally increase business with cross-selling efforts."**

As emerging technologies evolve, they raise the bar for possible questions. Consider these questions a sample for illustration and provocation purposes:

- How will blogs affect they way IT professionals conduct competitive analysis?
- What will blogs tell us about our customers and prospects?

- How can IT professionals understand trends and new behaviors from customer blogs?
- What will the impact of social networks be on the way IT professionals market products and services?
- How should we leverage the employees' network to sell?
- How do IT professionals nurture stratified customers for evangelism through social networks?
- What will be the new business model and compensation to members of the social networks who assist us in selling and promoting our products?
- How can we enhance the human aspect of our total customer experience by utilizing blogs and social networks?
- How should we capture and leverage customer voices as they are being shared in contact centers and retail stores?
- What customer behavior patterns can be captured through new wireless video technology?
- How can IT professionals leverage the audio and video technologies for better customer insight?
- How will available mobile technologies change the way we deliver our products?
- What new versions of our current services can we invent by using mobile technologies?

This list shows just a sample of the possible, yet necessary, disruptive questions that must emerge and be managed to ensure that information does not just provide answers but also triggers new thinking. Few have asked similar questions when the Internet and e-commerce emerged. Those who did managed to win and redefine their industries. If history is any indication of the future, we have again witnessed the reluctant behavior of big companies. Big companies, by dismissing those new technologies and sticking to their sources of information as proof that no significant change will occur, failed to ask disruptive questions. They instead used the information to subordinate the growth potential of their existing business models and shrink the great opportunities they faced into small and insignificant ones. Few companies use their information to ask new questions and define new business models.

By limiting the information role to incremental questions, IT professionals are not taking full advantage of the information they produce. They are handicapping their own organizations and not maximizing the value of their information technology investment. It is often the case that smaller and less-information-intensive start-up companies come up with new, innovative ways to create disruptions for the whole industry. Some examples are Amazon (the book business), Southwest Airlines and Jet Blue (the airline business), and Starbucks (the coffee-selling business).

This phenomenon can be explained by the handcuffs that companies put on their informa-

> " *By limiting the information role to incremental questions, IT professionals are not taking full advantage of the information they produce.* "

tion. When companies sit on top of a large pool of well-processed information, they use it for the wrong purpose: Rather than learn what should be the next big idea and the innovation gleaned from it, they use it to reinforce their existing operation and line of thinking. Rather than leverage the information to execute new ideas better and faster and in a less risky way, they leave the field open to companies without information who are willing to assume new risks for the great reward associated with it. Information is sent in order to sustain the current business rather than build a new one or bring the existing one to the next level through innovation. The misuse of information comes with the great risk of missing the next trends that will shore up the business. It also creates a void that often leads to the entry of new competitors, who then damage exactly the same business that you were trying to reaffirm and sustain.

REDEFINING CRM INFORMATION

By examining customer relationship management (CRM), the same pattern of focusing on incremental questions and avoiding order-of-magnitude questions can be discovered in a more specific case. Through building a robust customer database with analysis tools, the information is used to assist in incremental revenue growth of accessories. The information is used to reduce sales costs by introducing customer self-service alternatives. More information is gathered about customers to better understand their preferences, but this great source of information is unlikely to be used to examine how to change the business model altogether. Disruptive questions, such as "How do I build true partnership with customers" and "How do I manage customer insights and ideas," are not examined. "What other line of business should I start based on my customers' lifestyle changes and technology advancements?" "Can another unexplored question leverage the information in an innovative way?" The difference between these questions and the incremental questions IT professionals often ask is that the current ones have a low degree of disruption. Often, they know most of the answers already, and the information is merely a validation point. The business impact of incremental questions is likely to generate 10 percent to 15 percent in cost reduction or revenue growth.

> " More information is gathered about customers to better understand their preferences, but this great source of information is unlikely to be used to examine how to change the business model altogether "

Questions with a high degree of disruption also bear much greater potential. Although the incremental questions do not deliver differentiation and a competitive edge, disruptive questions do exactly that—they bear the potential of industry-altering practices, just as Amazon and eBay did. But these questions require a new way of thinking and processing the information. It requires an attitude of willingness to explore and get out of the comfort zone. It requires users to shift the role of information and to have a willingness to be exposed to change and something new rather than reside in the warm and cozy existing and known.

When you view the customer relationship management in a broader picture, it should not be just about managing and maximizing the existing relationship. It should include an element of redefining the relationship and evolving it with customers. Realizing the broader potential of customer relationship management, it allows companies to keep customers for life through an ongoing evolution of their value proposition. This evolution, however, will not materialize by repeating existing customer experiences. By providing consistently surprising experiences, rather than consistently providing the same experiences, companies keep their customers excited and interested. This approach requires the company to look at the collected customer data and the relationship management through a new set of lenses—lenses geared to value proposition and experiences, and to innovation, not repetition.

To achieve innovation-based customer relationship management, an ongoing process of creating new disruptive questions from the available information needs to be established. Companies need to develop brainstorming capabilities that challenge the information and channel it to the innovation process rather than to the affirming, reassuring process. As the owner of information, IT owns the challenge to build such mechanisms and educate users about how to take advantage of them and of the information they contain. It is the ultimate user experience. When the producer—in this case, IT—assumes the role of helping users maximize the value of its product, it ensures that the information product is utilized to its maximum capacity and delivers the maximum effect on the business.

BEST PRACTICES, PAST PRACTICES, AND NEXT PRACTICES

Benchmarks are about best practices, they say. They are assumed to be corporate shortcuts to excellence. Companies have been obsessed with best practices in the past decade, by attempting to match and copy other people's efficient operations. In reality, they are about *past* practices—the past practices of your competitors. Following them focuses on catching up to others, as opposed to leapfrogging them. While users are busy in benchmark matching, competitors are already leaping to the next best practice. They are creating the next practices.

Focusing on best practices diverts resources from innovating your own excellent practices. When employees are busy copying others, they have less time at hand to create something unique and new for their companies. They focus on activities that are anything but a competitive advantage. The same best practices that are available to you are available to your competition. Focusing on best practices

> " *Focusing on best practices diverts resources from innovating your own excellent practices.* "

means staying on par with the competition. At the end of the process, you will not achieve a single competitive edge because you are merely on par with the rest of the pack. Because many best practices are highly dependent on the specifics of the companies that invented them and therefore obtained the maximum value for them, they lose value and impact when applied to other companies. Because no company is 100 percent similar to another, a certain best practice in a given company (based on its specific core competency and dependencies), will be less applicable to a company with a different environment. When you adapt the best practices to your own environment, you dilute what used to be an excellent practice in one company and became an acceptable practice in yours.

As mentioned earlier, you conduct all these efforts at the expense of your ability to innovate and create your own practices. They will not be best practices, but, rather, next practices. Following trends and others' practices is following someone else's agenda. Often, whenever you're following an agenda, you do not fully understand because you did not create it. Doing this results in unoriginal execution, dilution, and a loss of the splendor caused by the virtue of copying. No customer will pay a premium for a copy. She will seek the original. Creating originals is impossible if information is being used for answers. Originals are the result of people facing information, but coming up with questions that lead to seeing the information beyond the obvious.

Following best practices is another shortcut that leaves the internally developed information untouched and runs to leverage the needs of others. Getting out of the commoditization rut that is plaguing most organizations today requires innovation in business practices as well as in product innovation. When leveraged to ask high-degree disruptive questions, information can play a critical role in developing not the best practices, but, rather, the next practices. I am not referring to the practices that will get your business on par with the competition, but, rather, the ones that will catch them off guard as you will redefine the rules. The concept of innovative next practices is about playing by your own rules. It is about creating and selling an original. Originals might be risky, but they bear better results that justify the risk.

Being like everyone else is about best practices. Following others or playing by someone else's rules is not a recommended long-term strategy. It is the innovators with the next practices who collect the larger share of business and market. Order-of magnitude-growth does not often come from copying others or from following an agenda set by a competitor. This type of growth comes from charting your own path and forcing others to follow you.

8

The Innovation Platform: Turning Information into Action

"Imagination is more important than knowledge. Knowledge is limited. Imagination encircles the world."

Albert Einstein

THE INNOVATION FOUNDATION: ENABLING USER INNOVATION

Suppose that several of your users have come up with ideas. Each one has independently observed a business process and come up with a way to improve it. Suppose that a customer makes a phone call to your contact center and proposes a new way to use your product. How do you capture these insights?

What happens to the myriad of great and not-so-great ideas that are evolving in your business? What is the mechanism to collect and assess them and ultimately drive execution?

The vast majority of companies talk about innovating, but lack the tools and platform to manage this process. In fact, IT and its systems are often regarded as anti-innovation—the creativity busters. Because the systems utilize process-based and not innovation-based technologies, they are considered rigid and inflexible. Users complain that new ideas and changes often face IT objections and rejections, and they claim that the required adaptations will take a long time and bear a hefty price tag. Users either give up their ideas or implement them only partly and at the slow IT pace, thus losing market advantage. Or, they find ways to bypass IT and get the job done on their own. Neither option is complementary to IT's capabilities.

> **" The vast majority of companies talk about innovating, but lack the tools and platform to manage this process. "**

It is time to design and implement an innovation platform that allows users to act on their ideas and transform them—at the market pace, not at the IT pace—into commercial reality. Unlike previous efforts, such as home-grown applications created internally or system integrators, this proposed platform must be designed completely from users' experiences.

For years, companies invested in custom-made applications, also known as home-grown applications, that were meant to address their special needs. Those applications were designed to specifications and followed a specific function, interaction, or process and were designed to complement the process. Users were considered subservient to the process and not primary to it. Then, as an afterthought, the applications required a "prettier" user interface. Designing around the user experience was considered "nice to have," and most system integrators and internal IT people regarded it as a nuisance and not as a core competency. The result was disgruntled users who reluctantly complied with the new applications designed based on process-focus. Users never bothered to embrace the applications or take full advantage of their capabilities. Additionally, these home-grown applications were too isolated and not connected to the rest of the organization's operation, which resulted in long-term abandonment. Combined with the applications' high maintenance costs and the fact that they were not easily sharing information with other parts of the organizations, they were eventually discarded. Companies were seeking technology platforms that seamlessly communicated and were more interconnected.

The proposed innovation platform differs from those home-grown applications in several ways. User-centricity gives them a "heads' up" over home-grown applications. By being user-centric, they ensure greater flexibility and user acceptance and utilization. Leveraging the innovation platform, which is consistent across the whole organization, will enable the faster, more flexible, and more cost-effective creation of applications. The utilization of a common platform base with access to multiple sources of information and users creates a common denominator that is desperately missing in custom-made applications. The innovation platform is not an isolated tool, but is a common ground for cooperation across the entire organization.

> " *Leveraging the innovation platform, which is consistent across the whole organization, will enable the faster, more flexible, and more cost-effective creation of applications.* "

THE USER-CENTRIC INNOVATION PLATFORM

For users to take full advantage of the innovation platform, it has to be designed in accordance with their behavior and consumption of information. The platform must fit their lifestyle rather than be foreign to it.

Designing a user-centric innovation platform should take into consideration these guidelines:

- **Understand users' lifestyles.** Recognize what their lives look like and what their task responsibilities and priorities are. Users' business issues and lifestyles should dictate platform design. Mobile users behave differently from office-based users who have ongoing access to computers and portals. Business builders have different worries and considerations than churners, who have different tasks and agendas on their minds. By adapting to user behavior patterns and lifestyles, IT can ensure greater acceptance as they reduce user adaptations and learning curve costs. Greater user utilization of information will affect their value to the organization.

- **Identify consumption and interaction patterns.** Focus on the "chemistry" between users and information. Some of those interaction patterns have disastrous results, and others enjoy great relationships. Understanding that information alone is insufficient because the shift must take place in order to focus on the chemistry with users. It is necessary to see the information world from the users perspective. How do they consume information? How much time do they dedicate to it? What are their search methods? What are they missing? Combined with users' business agendas, adapting to user consumption and interaction with information is critical to developing a platform that truly drives greater information utilization.

> " For users to take full advantage of the innovation platform, it has to be designed in accordance with their behavior and consumption of information. "

- **Give everyone access.** Organizations no longer have the privilege of allowing access to information only to people on their payrolls. Companies are too dependent on outside users, such as partners, suppliers, dealers, and customers who contribute to the information creation and utilization process. Any innovation process must take this principle into account. Although information integrity and confidentiality must be retained, users from all over a company's ecosystem will be accessing information. The innovation platform ought to accommodate that fact. IT needs to start accepting the fact that IT serves a greater set of users than just those who are on the company payroll.

- **Provide information anywhere.** The platform should include the ability to access information from anywhere. Limiting availability limits usage. In an ever more mobile world, users need to access their information anywhere they live or conduct business. Make the information available at a user's place. Information security systems must be adapted and mobile users and information consumption from remote sites accommodated. If your organization has plant workers without access to a computer, consider kiosks where they can access information more easily on the plant floor. If your service people are mobile and spending 80 percent or more of their time with customers, consider providing the service people with powerful mobile devices with full access. Information must be where users are.

- **Provide proactive information.** Information can no longer be passive. Waiting in a portal to be redeemed by the few users who will find it is a verdict for irrelevance. The information ought to be proactive. Users should be alerted to updates in the relevant information based on their business agendas. Catching up with users rather than users catching up with customers is the future of useful information. The rest is doomed to be ignored.

- **Make the process collaborative.** To make information useful, users should be able to share it and obtain opinions and suggestions from others. The innovation platform should reflect this need with collaborative tools that allow faster collaboration and more cost-effective collaboration. Doing this will also support the decision process and enable users to reduce their decisions' risks and obtain greater acceptance faster.
- **Put information into context.** From a user's perspective, unless the information is presented in context, it is useless. Facing a growing amount of external and competitive information, users need to be able to compare and contrast the variety of sources. Otherwise, each user is isolated and as such not useful to the overall decision. Presenting information to users in context focuses on accumulating multiple sources of information, both internal and external, and delivering them to users in a processed way that allows them to make decisions.

PART I: USER IDENTITY AND ACCESS MANAGEMENT

Designing an innovation platform from the user perspective requires building a unified user repository. Both internal users and authorized external users, such as suppliers, customers, and channel partners, should be included in a centralized repository of users. This unified repository is then connected to multiple sources of information to allow authorized access by the users listed in the repository.

By aligning the centralized repository with the sources of information, a company eliminates the waste of multiple passwords and the notorious delays in access caused by the replication and complexity associated with managing all isolated sources of information. Eliminating multiple passwords is a major step toward adapting a user's perspective, because password changes are one of the costly items on any

> " *Eliminating multiple passwords is a major step toward adapting a user's perspective, because password changes are one of the costly items on any IT help desk.* "

IT help desk. The simplification of one password with access to all authorized information is bound to increase user satisfaction and utilization
while lowering the cost of obtaining information.

Following the connection between the repository and the sources
of information, another layer of access and usage privileges will be
added. Based on their business responsibilities and agendas, users can
then be assigned usage privileges and access to allow them to quickly
reach the right information wherever it is. While one user will be
allowed to view only certain information, another will be allowed to
modify it. Providing this level of agility allows a company to deliver the
right access to each user without compromising information integrity.
It usually increases access authorization because of the ability to control
the nature of each user's usage and prevents the abuse of information by
unauthorized users.

Identity and access management are a critical first step toward a
user-centric innovation platform. They allow faster and easier access
management by users. New users can take advantage of the information
they need in a matter of minutes, not weeks, as is the traditional way.
Reorganizations will no longer pose a challenge because IT will be able
to adapt access privileges fast. Suppliers and other outside users will be
allowed access to the internal information without compromising the
information's integrity. Departing users will be eliminated from the list
in a matter of minutes, rather than weeks or sometimes months, thus
preventing the common potential of compromising information
integrity.

Building an identity-and-access management tool as part of the
innovation platform has its financial rewards. The most important reward
is that as an adaptable, user-centric tool, it is bound to increase information utilization and empower users to make intelligent decisions.

PART II: THE ORGANIZATION SERVICES PLATFORM

Following user identity and access management, the organization service platform is the next component required in the innovation platform. Considering the complexity and sheer number of information
sources, the organization service platform (OSP) is geared toward the
consolidation and prioritization of information to make it more useful

and actionable. The organization service platform includes these three elements:

- People integration
- Information integration
- Process integration

The platform includes connectivity to existing enterprise applications, such as customer relationship management (CRM), financial applications, enterprise resource planning (ERP), and supplier relationship management (SRM). The platform collects information from everywhere and provides it to users. Being able to connect all existing information into one platform simplifies information access for users and ensures that they obtain all available information.

> " *Considering the complexity and sheer number of information sources, the organization service platform (OSP) is geared toward the consolidation and prioritization of information to make it more useful and actionable.* "

To be truly user-centric, the organization service platform should adapt to user behavior. Information access has to be made easy and fast and be done through a common interface. If users have to struggle to obtain information, they will not bother. Inaccessible information is non-existent information and is therefore unusable, from the user's perspective. Strong, user-friendly search capabilities can transform confusing, unused data into a forceful and highly utilized source of knowledge. The organization service platform must reflect user behavior and information-consumption styles to ensure that the information that is delivered is utilized.

By adding knowledge management and business intelligence, the organization service platform then moves toward processing the information, placing it in context and enabling users to see it in a holistic way. These strategies are critical to the processing of information because they add context value that allows users to prioritize and assign importance to the wide variety of available information sources.

Complementing the processed and prioritized information with collaboration and messaging capabilities now allows users to share information and enhance its value through the insight of others. Internal colleagues or external suppliers, customers, and other important stake-holders can now add more value and expedite the decision-making process. Their added value will also ensure the completeness of the decision because it takes into account multiple dimensions and needs. The collaboration also decreases the change-management costs associated with the decision and ensure its readiness for execution. The more collaborators and users can add to the process, the better the decision will be and the faster it will be executed.

The organization service platform has to enable the creation of a whole new host of applications. At the end of the process, it is those flexible applications that need to run on the platform and conduct business processes more effectively and quickly. The business intelligence and the portal capabilities are enablers within the application's function. The difference, however, from previous monolithic applications is that the applications working as part of the organization service platform are all modules. They are modular and flexible and subject to change and adaptation as quickly as necessary based on changing needs. Freed from the need to connect to users and information, which is already provided by other platform components, the modular applications focus instead on functionality and the ability to adapt. These modular applications, freed from the need to create a monolithic food chain, are more adaptable to changing requirements, business structures, partner and customer needs, and the overall competitive landscape. They usher in an era of applications whose creation until now were not justified on their own. If a certain business process was not significant enough to justify a supporting application, it usually was subjugated to one of the larger in-house applications, such as Customer Relationship Management (CRM) or Enterprise Resource Planning (ERP). Another alternative was to conduct the business process on spreadsheets and other primitive, home-grown solutions. A framework for application development is therefore an important component of the platform. This will allow organizations to craft their needed applications rapidly and easily and will enable them to respond to different and, often, conflicting requirements. A development framework will bring the development capabilities in-house and will reduce costs and dependency while shortening response time.

Mobility plays an important role in the innovation process. Allowing collaboration and execution from anywhere is a must for users. Recent developments in mobile technology, such as standardization,

WiFi technology, and more powerful devices, facilitate the mobility level that users crave. IT needs to ensure that its innovation platform includes a powerful mobility aspect that allows users the freedom of collaboration and execution anywhere, based on user behavior, location, and importance to the business. Users should be able to be empowered with the right device that can deliver the required information and capabilities. This freedom is critical to users as they become more mobile than ever and are required to spend more time in the field and in front of customers.

When a new business process is formulated through a new modular application, a life cycle management is required in order to complement it. Managing aspects such as introduction, change, and adaptation management and implementation are part of life cycle management. This supporting tool will enable IT to maximize the value of the modular applications not only during introduction, but also throughout the life cycle of the project or process they support. Adaptations and changes that until now were not possible because of high costs are a natural part of the organization services platform and therefore should be managed and implemented. The life cycle management tool should enable IT to maximize the value of those applications all the way to retirement through disposability or recycling options.

When designing the organization services platform, certain abilities should not be forgotten or taken for granted. The abstraction of hardware and operating systems is critical. The platform should know how to handle a heterogeneous environment and be agnostic to the underlying layer of operating systems and hardware. Complementing the heterogeneous environment in most IT operations is critical to its feasibility. Other critical aspects include platform security. Flexibility should not come at the expense of security. The openness and adaptability of the organization service platform puts it at risk to greater penetration and exposure. The consolidation of all users and making all information easily accessible makes the information easy prey for criminal minds. The security element of the platform must adapt to that level of openness and information access. Scalability is another critical aspect. The platform is not a tool for a few users. It is an enterprise-wide investment that should be ready to service users and collaborators around the world. It should also be able to mirror and respond to a company's evolving growth goals, such as mergers and acquisitions. As such, scalability is not an option, but is a necessity. Reliability and stability are other aspects of the platform that are often hard to measure but are critical to performance. When building the organization service platform, IT has to adhere to its name as a service platform for the whole organization. IT should develop tools to examine scalability and reliability before introducing them to the company to ensure that they live up to expectations and demands.

The complete innovation platform, combining user identity and access management with information integration and a processing platform that assembles, processes, and communicates the information gives users new the freedom to explore fresh ideas. The cost of new ideas will be reduced dramatically. At the same time, the time to value will increase because users can implement ideas faster and in a more cost-effective way than ever. The innovation platform will then become an accelerator of their innovation efforts. Adapting to the user behavior and lifestyles will allow IT, for the first time, to enable users and not just enable abstract processes. Users will no longer be subservient to a "greater-than-them" process, but will be the driver for the technology. Users are at the center of the innovation platform, and the technology is at their service, not the other way around.

INNOVATION DEMOCRATIZATION

When IT realizes that ideas happen everywhere, the need to capture them and evaluate them becomes critical. It is the lifeblood of an organization's future. Without these innovative ideas, no business can move forward. Without moving forward, they are bound to move backward as their competitors leap to the next big thing. Status quo is not an option in business. Because businesses live in an ecosystem with competitors and customer preferences that are constantly changing, they are more dependent than ever on the ideas of their employees and customers. Because ideas happen simultaneously everywhere in an organization, the innovation process must be democratized.

> " When IT realizes that ideas happen everywhere, the need to capture them and evaluate them becomes critical. It is the lifeblood of an organization's future. "

Regardless of rank or seniority, every idea must get a fair chance and a full evaluation. Companies should nurture environments in which people are not afraid to speak their minds and do not fear reprimand. Often, corporate culture, especially one that uses information for reaffirmation, does not lend itself to innovative thinking. Employees fearing ridicule act as rubber stamps for their superiors' ideas and thoughts and hold back their innovative thoughts. Others are afraid to take risks because they fear the repercussions. They then assume similar behavior and keep their thoughts away from the limelight. Both behaviors rob an organization of critical intellectual property being created at the company, and the company cannot take advantage of it.

Democratizing the process is about nurturing a culture in which mistakes are a part of doing business. Mistakes might even be rewarded because they are attempts at innovation, and the willingness to take risks is appreciated. The innovation democratization process is about opening innovation to everyone in an organization and judging ideas on merit and business value rather than on the person's ranking.

When Whirlpool developed an innovation platform, it trained and provided access to 10,000 employees. By creating such a critical mass of innovators, the company was able to generate 7,500 new ideas, and 360 of them reached the pilot stage. Democratizing the innovation process combined with effective tools and training resulted in building the future of the company on a more solid base with a much larger pool of growth opportunities and, as such, a better-managed risk. Democratizing the innovation process and applying a systematic approach to capturing and evaluating it leads organizations to an overall more solid business operation. Organizations no longer count on a few select geniuses to land the next big idea. Instead, they count on a much larger pool of people with a significantly greater probability of idea generation. A larger pool of ideas means better risk management and better choices for growth. The dependency on a single great idea with all the risk associated with such behavior is eliminated from the equation.

Democratizing the innovation process sends a great message to employees and encourages them to participate. Companies, on their part, need to complement the training and innovation process with compensation and incentive plans that share the commercial impact of the ideas with those who generated them. Without it, employees will be reluctant to share their brainpower because some will opt out to establish their own businesses and reap the full benefits of their ideas. A powerful incentive program can assist in keeping these great ideas in-house and leveraging the benefits of those ideas internally.

SELLING INFORMATION TO USERS: WHAT IS IN IT FOR ME?

"Users are resistant to change and technology" is a common claim among IT organizations. They tend to blame their users for their reluctance to adopt the latest versions of applications imposed on them. At the same time, however, those same reluctant users of technology download new applications and games from Internet sites without permission. They also started using instant messaging long before corporate IT was ready to deal with it. How do IT professionals resolve this reluctance to use some technologies with the early adoption of other technologies among the same users? The answer is simple: by selling, educating, and mentoring. With the complete dissemination approach, users will make the effort to adopt technologies that were "sold" to them (sometimes after leaping great hurdles, such as corporate IT guidelines). On the other hand, technologies that were imposed on them with no "selling" will face great resistance.

As part of a user-centric organization, IT must adopt the role of sellers, not just providers. They must help users understand and get excited about the information so that they buy into using it. It is often amazing to see millions of dollars spent on a new technology or application, and hardly any money spent on user change management and buy-in. It is always assumed that users will just adapt automatically. In reality, neglecting the selling efforts will result in significant costs, ranging from delayed implementations to cancellations of entire projects. According to Gartner research, it is expected that by 2007 approximately 50 percent of CRM projects will be considered a failure by the companies who attempted

> **" As part of a user-centric organization, IT must adopt the role of sellers, not just providers. They must help users understand and get excited about the information so that they buy into using it. "**

to implement them. Failure to "sell" to users accelerates the possibility of failure and increases overall implementation costs.

As owners of the information product, IT professionals must adapt themselves to the role of salespeople and engage with users as customers, not as captive audience members required to swallow whatever they are being fed.

Selling is a skill set that most IT professionals do not associate themselves with. It is not what professional IT people typically do because their technology should stand on its own. For many IT professionals, the concept of selling is rather difficult and challenging. IT professionals, perceiving themselves as professional technologists, look on selling as an inferior trade for other, more "lowly" people. It is what salespeople do to their customers. In today's environment, everyone needs to sell an idea in order to advance his or her own agenda. Selling is a tool of the trade of every successful businessperson. The origin of the word *sale* comes from an ancient Scandinavian dialect and means *selzig,* or service. If IT professionals would relate to selling in its original meaning, they might be more comfortable in assuming the selling role. Servicing users and enabling them to reach and exceed their business objectives through information-based services is the essence of selling to them. Unfortunately, many users will not be serviced without being "sold" first, which seems to be a prerequisite in a world full of endless marketing and messaging assaults. Users need to understand the value of the proposed service in order to allocate attention and resources to it. So, selling is, after all, another form of serving customers. It is serving them with the knowledge to make their operations effective and their decisions smarter. It is empowering them to become more productive in their businesses. But selling becomes an increasingly important skill that everyone in a company must master. If IT has any hope for better user cooperation, selling will be the critical skill that will assist in this transition.

Tools, on their own, do not get the job done. Just like with a pile of wood, a saw and a hammer cannot build a dining room set on their own. It is people who breathe life into the potential tools and use them to create great things. Selling to users focuses on making them want to cooperate. It is the replacement of ordering or forcing users to act, which are archaic methods that have failed to obtain true acceptance and cooperation. Users cannot be coerced to cooperate. Resolution is no longer a matter of receiving "please cooperate" memos from the CEO. Selling focuses on persuading users, by explaining, coaching, convincing, and, ultimately, making them want to do something and think that it is their idea to cooperate.

IT must "sell" users on technologies, applications, and information, if it wants users to cooperate and "buy" their products. On their own, technologies, applications, and information do not mean much. When users take advantage of them, they become major business enablers. For years, IT's engagement with users was limited to a brief requirement definition and application training. But the complete ownership of their technology and information success was owned by no one. IT professionals assumed that it was up to users to own these elements; users, of course, associated the success with the technology and, consequently, expected IT to take care of it. It is not important to solve the question of who is right. What is important is that if IT truly cares for information utilization, it will have to start selling.

ACCELERATING ACCEPTANCE AND COOPERATION

The purpose of sales efforts is not to add complexity to the IT effort. It is instead a tool for IT to achieve its objectives. An effective sales campaign will allow IT to accelerate technology acceptance and information utilization. Better user understanding of the value of the technology and its information ensures higher user utilization, which makes it achieve their goals.

> " Better user understanding of the value of the technology and its information ensures higher user utilization, which makes it achieve their goals. "

Despite its traditionally negative reputation, selling is a critical tool to obtain cooperation. Users and people in general do not just follow orders because they were told to do so. Policies and procedures are no longer an effective way to enforce cooperation and ensure compliance. Selling and persuasion are replacing the old enforcement method in encouraging users to cooperate with new initiatives. The objective of persuasion is to educate users about why the new technologies or initiatives are good for them. Unlike enforcement through procedures and compliance, through policies that constitute an external agenda to users and as such are always in conflict with their personal agendas, selling acts in a completely different way. By providing reasons and logic, and not just orders, selling leverages on the users' internal wants and wishes. It transforms the requested cooperation to users' agendas and therefore makes them more prone to do what IT wants them to do. Effective selling makes users want what the seller wants them to want. It is a completely different level of communication.

Addressing the need for selling and rejecting the traditional negative connotation of selling will be an important first step for IT to adjust to its new role. Installing technology or providing application training no longer makes the cut in users' ever busier and more crowded world. They will, at best, reluctantly use the new technologies, but do so with minimal interest and therefore minimal results.

Selling to users focuses on elevating the new technologies and information to the level of users' priorities and interests and drives better utilization and results. To do so, IT needs to acquire new selling and persuasion skills and understand the dynamics of selling and how to craft an effective selling campaign.

DESIGNING A SALES CAMPAIGN

Although I am not attempting to replace the hundreds of sales training and coaching books, few guidelines are required in order to provide a head start for any IT professional. Moreover, because selling the value of technology to users is not a typically covered subject in most sales books, the guidelines in this section will be beneficial to understand the nature of the required sales skills and programs.

Bombarded with ever-growing advertising messages, the average customer in the Western world is exposed to between 3,000 and 5,000 messages a day, according to several sources. As such, his attention span is short and the customer's ability to digest the messages effectively is diminishing. Creating an effective communication program will require a punchy campaign that draws attention quickly. In facing a new proposition, a customer requires the answer to these questions:

- Why should I care?
- So what?
- What is in it for me?

- What do I have to change in my routine?
- How does it threaten me or my lifestyle?
- How do I use it?
- Can you prove it?

Without concrete answers to these questions, there is no customer attention. The answers must be persuasive and not generic, and they had better be supported by measurable results and undisputed supporting proof because customers are ever more skeptical and are trained to detect "fluff" answers that are untrue or not provable.

Being able to address these questions effectively and quickly is critical to winning users' hearts and cooperation. As you can see from this list of questions, users do not care about the features, just as they do not care about what saw was used to construct a dining room set. For users, the features are tools—nothing more than that. Users care about and focus on results. What do the tools or features do for them, and how do they solve their business problems? IT professionals are experts in explaining feature functionality. They are not experts in applying features to business problems and to a user's world of issues and challenges. This is, however, the essence of selling.

> ❝ Users often ignore new technology tools and continue to use their archaic system of spreadsheets to run critical business functions. They do so because they find the technology threatening. ❞

The issue of threatening changes is especially acute when IT sells to users. Users often ignore new technology tools and continue to use their archaic system of spreadsheets to run critical business functions. They do so because they find the technology threatening. For IT professionals, technology is never threatening. Version upgrades are common, and the technology world in general is full of new solutions and technologies, from new start-ups and existing companies. Change is a constant in technology, and IT is accustomed to it. Average users, on the other hand, are anything but ready for change. They are not exposed to this level of fast-paced change and are therefore not comfortable with it. They have also not seen or heard about technologies that help reduce the amount of manual work done by people or eliminate it altogether. IT professionals are used to technology-driven advancement and cutting-edge practices. Users view it as a tool to eliminate employees. Combine this lack of exposure to fast change with the fear of elimination, and the concept of threat makes more sense.

IT professionals must address this issue head-on immediately and not wait to be asked. Most likely, they will not be asked because users keep their thoughts to themselves. Just because users do not ask does not mean that they are not thinking about it. In designing a sales campaign, the issue of technology threats and consequences should be addressed proactively. By doing so, you respond to the unexpressed fears of users.

Selling and persuasion focus on making other people do what you want them to do. In the technology context, they accelerate the acceptance of new information and tools. IT, by using effective selling tools, will be able to breathe life into its implemented tools and produce the right information for the right people who will then take advantage of the information to drive business impact. Without selling, IT is left with a pile of partially to totally unutilized tools and a big hole in their budgets. With selling, the IT investment is maximized, information is utilized, and new revenues evolve to enrich companies.

9

Information as Change Accelerator

"I don't think much of a man who is not wiser today than he was yesterday."

Abraham Lincoln

SEEING INFORMATION AS THE CHANGE ACCELERATOR

Information can play a major role in accelerating change in organizations rather than delaying it. Today, however, IT is often regarded as a change delayer. Rigid processes and applications combined with an attitude of "It cannot be done" or "It will take a year" often causes IT to be perceived by users as the anti-innovation and anti-creativity group. This perception can be changed, but only if IT assumes the role of change accelerator.

By viewing its role from the perspective of users' experience, IT can see opportunities in accelerating projects and change in organizations. The challenge for IT is not only to erase the bad reputation of the rigid-processes people and the enforcer of policies, but also to leap into a new role. Shedding its anti-innovation reputation will be insufficient because it will still not connect IT to the organization's mainstream growth agenda. Leaping to change acceleration is the challenge at hand. It means not only shedding an old reputation, but also creating a new one by enabling faster change and supporting the way users conduct their business.

Combining an innovation platform with user management by studying and reinventing the way users make decisions will position IT to accelerate innovation and support it. The contribution of IT to thoroughly infuse relevant, complete, and actionable information through the innovation process will affect the organization and its ability to move faster and retain a cutting-edge position in the market. This cutting edge will be translated into the ability to retain a larger market share, obtain a premium price for products and services, and extend the length of relationships with customers, all of

> *" Combining an innovation platform with user management by studying and reinventing the way users make decisions will position IT to accelerate innovation and support it. "*

which, in return, reduces the cost of selling.

This information-based innovation affects users and their decisions in several ways, as described in the following sections.

COLLABORATING WITH DIVERSE PARTICIPANTS

Because innovation requires diversity, the collaboration aspect of the innovation platform combined with user management will enable faster, affordable collaboration between users from different parts of an organization. Time zones and geographical distances will be reduced dramatically and with them the costs associated with those distances.

"Our vision is that 50 percent of all P&G discovery and invention could come from outside the company." This ambitious target was set by Procter & Gamble CEO Allan G. Lafley in 2002, when only 20 percent of P&G innovation came from the outside. This ambition also required a platform to support it. Allowing outsiders such as start-ups, university researchers, suppliers, and sometimes competitors into the organization's core innovation required the facilitation of new users who are not part of the payroll and do not report to the CEO. It required a tool to protect internal proprietary information while allowing an abundance of

access to relevant information. It posed a new challenge for collaboration that demanded an innovation platform.

With the innovation platform, external and internal users are no
longer a threat, but rather an opportunity. Users can now collaborate
faster and reach better decisions and achieve both faster time to market
and greater time to value through maximizing decisions and innovating
through diverse collaboration. Decisions and opportunities can be evaluated and capitalized on at the market pace and not at the organizational weakest-link pace. If collaboration before the platform was
implemented was costly and delayed because of people's availability, after
the innovation platform was implemented, these issues are eliminated.
Limitations to internal users will be lifted because external users can be
ushered into the innovation process without compromising internal
resources and confidential information. All participants are given access
to the information they require for the innovation process, but prohib-
ited from accessing unnecessary information. Regardless of their
locations, people can participate effectively and contribute to the
process in a timely manner to ensure that no opportunity will be lost or miss its window of
opportunity.

> " With the innovation platform, external and internal users are no longer a threat, but rather an opportunity. "

REDUCING THE COSTS OF NEW IDEA IMPLEMENTATION: USHERING IN MORE INNOVATIONS

One of the most significant benefits of the investment in an innovation
platform and democratizing the innovation process is the lesser amount
of time involved in the introduction of new ideas. Ideas that were costly
to evaluate or implement are now feasible. The innovation platform can
now enable an affordable evaluation process with the cost of information
and validation significantly reduced. Users can also provide more complete execution guidelines, design marketing, and go-to-market strategies
faster because of the availability of complete relevant information.

The information-based innovation platform allows users to usher in
innovations and ideas that otherwise would have been lost. Ideas that were
not considered before, because of the cost of evaluation, often represented
missed opportunities. These could have been opportunities that a company

could afford to miss in today's cutthroat environment, where the life spans of new products and competitive edges are even more limited. Enabling innovation that until now was not possible positions IT in a completely different role as revenue enablers, not cost crunchers. It also turns users into heroes and allows them to build their businesses.

> " *In a twisted way, the traditional cost-reduction role of IT is coming back, but in the context of innovation-driven revenue generation.* "

In a twisted way, the traditional cost-reduction role of IT is coming back, but in the context of innovation-driven revenue generation. From the business perspective, this effect is different: it is the type of effect that transforms IT into the organization's mainstream agenda.

PRIORITIZING INFORMATION: INTELLIGENT DECISIONS

By allowing users to understand the conflicting sets of information they face, the innovation platform allows them to make smarter decisions. Prioritization decisions or implementation decisions require both a complete set of available information and better insight to drive the right decisions. Great ideas can fall on wrong implementation decisions. Missing the right piece of information might lead to an oversight and lost opportunity. Companies can no longer afford to lose opportunities to competitors or new start-ups.

> " *The quality of user decisions and, therefore, business performance is highly dependent on the completeness, quality, relevance, and timeliness of infomation in the innovation platform.* "

The ability to consolidate and process information to provide knowledge and insight to users in real-time is the essence of the ability to compete today. IT has a crucial role to play in this process, through its information. The quality of user decisions and, therefore, business performance is highly dependent on the completeness, quality, relevance, and timeliness of information in the innovation platform.

FASTER IMPLEMENTATION
AND PROCESS FORMATION

During the selection process, ideas are evaluated, among other factors, on the size of the opportunity as well as the cost of bringing them to market. The innovation platform has a unique value in enabling faster and affordable application creation that speeds up the product or service introduction. Allowing users to leverage an existing set of information and processes will enable them to accept ideas that otherwise would have been rejected because of the cost of creation and market introduction.

Following the decision to select a certain innovative idea, execution becomes critical. The speed of execution is important because users do not know who they might compete against. The possibility always exists in the never-ending competitive race that an entrepreneur or a competitor somewhere is working on the same idea. Therefore, time to market becomes an issue in order to maximize an opportunity's potential.

> " The speed of execution is important because users do not know who they might compete against. The possibility always exists in the never-ending competitive race that an entrepreneur or a competitor somewhere is working on the same idea. "

The innovation platform should allow the faster implementation of processes through customized applications created faster for that purpose. By leveraging available users, information, and processes in the innovation platform, applications can now be customized at a much faster pace and in a much more affordable way to enable speedy execution.

ACCELERATING INTEGRATION

Another value is the acceleration of cooperation with outside companies. Mergers and acquisitions are notoriously difficult and costly because of conflicting systems and user resistance. Organizations that deal with mergers and acquisitions usually are forced into lengthy and costly processes to integrate the two entities. This process takes years and faces many hurdles that sometimes result in obtaining no real synergy. By utilizing innovation platforms, users can be provided with tools for collaboration and fast access to information. This can reduce the time to value of the acquisition. The innovation platform has the potential to affect mergers and acquisitions in several ways, including making them happen, reducing the cycle of integration, and reducing the costs associated with them.

THE DISPOSABLE APPLICATION

The traditional costs of applications and technologies made many of them cost prohibitive and therefore not useful in certain projects. By leveraging an innovation platform, small innovation-supporting applications can be created with more cost effectiveness. As such, a new era of the disposable application has arrived. Because of the reusability of the innovation platform, users might create new applications just for temporary use for a certain project or campaign. The cost of creation is low, and therefore the application can be justified. But, following a successful implementation, the application might not be used any more. The company will not bear the maintenance costs and might dispose of it.

Users, for their part, knowing that the costs of applications are significantly lower because of the existence of the innovation platform, might justify the creation of a disposable application. IT, knowing that the core of the information, users, and processes remained within the innovation platform, might justify discarding the application and forgo unnecessary maintenance costs.

Disposable applications might be a legitimate solution for certain projects and one-time programs. Today, they might exist in Excel spreadsheets or on paper because disposable applications are too costly. With the innovation platform, however, a new era of disposable applications might be ushered in. These applications are easy and fast to create, respond to a one-time need, and are ready to be discarded after their use is completed.

THE RECYCLABLE APPLICATION

Another manifestation of the flexible application is the recyclable application. Consider an application that was designed for a clinical trial in a pharmaceutical company. The application leveraged the infrastructure of users and information, but had specific functions developed for the trial. Following the trial, the application became obsolete because the company did not need it any more. But, what is obsolete for one company might be quite beneficial for another. The application, without users and information, can be offered as a recyclable application to other companies in the market. Other companies might find the defined set of capabilities of the applications valuable and a way to shorten their business cycle and overall project costs. Therefore, they might choose to purchase the application. The application at that point will be well tested, free of bugs, and ready to run faster on another company's infrastructure of users and information. A few modifications and corrections might be required, but, otherwise, the purchasing company will be up and running faster, with a tailored application that otherwise would have cost five times as much, if not more, to create from scratch.

> " A few modifications and corrections might be required, but, otherwise, the purchasing company will be up and running faster, with a tailored application that otherwise would have cost five times as much, if not more, to create from scratch. "

For the selling company, the recyclability of the application can be a driver to justify certain projects and to reduce their overall costs. Now, applications that otherwise could not have been justified are ready to go, knowing that there is a residual value to their IT development efforts. Justifying those applications will then affect the ability to execute the projects faster and more effectively and help them gain a competitive advantage in the marketplace. The recyclable application opens new opportunities for IT investments to be maximized and justified.

FACILITATING COMMUNICATION TO REDUCE CHANGE MANAGEMENT COSTS

An integral part of any new product or service is change management. Multiple internal and external stakeholders are involved in the success of the defined opportunity. Each one needs to be informed and needs to get ready for its part. Communication with all stakeholders is costly and challenging. Even the well-selected new products and the ones that were well executed during the implementation stage fail on communication and change management. The collaborative nature of the innovation platform and its ability to reach multiple users allows users to leverage them to design effective and successful change management campaigns. Stakeholders from around the world and across different functions are immediately informed through a tier-preferred method of communication. Communication is interactive, not one-sided, and as such allows stakeholders to take an active role, cooperate, and assume responsibility for success.

Keeping stakeholders informed and engaged without the time-consuming efforts traditionally associated with such tasks expedites the innovation time to market.

BEATING THE LAW OF SIZE

In his book *The Judo Strategy,* Professor Avraham Yoffie describes the bureaucratic weight that holds back companies. The companies he describes in terms of sumo wrestlers are held back by their legacy of business and are unable to respond to market changes as fast as their start-up counterparts do. The start-ups, which are described in terms of judo wrestlers, are agile and fast and take advantage of their lack of weight to perform much faster and capitalize on opportunities that the sumo companies are too slow to capture. According to Yoffie, these inherent limitations position sumo-type companies to enter late to market and act as followers rather than as innovators. In his book *The Innovator's Dilemma,* Prof. Clayton M. Christensen echoes similar ideas. He argues that the success of current products blinds innovators from seeing the next big trend and adapting to it. By focusing on enhancing and fine-tuning their current successes, they are too distracted to pay attention to market dynamics. By failing to notice them, they allow competitors large and small to redefine their market conditions and rival them into obsolescence.

Part of the trap lies in the fact that when new markets emerge, they are too small to be pursued by large companies. Often, the total size of an emerging market will be equal to a statistical error in the large company's balance sheet. There will therefore be no justification to pursue the new idea at that stage. By the time the market grows to a respectable size, it is already occupied by start-up companies that assumed the risk and found it rewarding early in the growth stage and that are now positioned as market leaders. At this stage, many of the sumo-like companies face a well-defined market need in which they arrive too late. They have the option of innovation, but it will be a following act rather than true innovation. Some large players managed to dominate markets after arriving late into them. Pulling their size and ability to reduce costs, they became cost leaders rather than innovators. Their market share is derived from the no-premium customers who did not expect any innovation. They are often positioned for accelerated commoditization. The other alternative is to pay a hefty price for a hyped start-up as their expensive ticket into the market.

> " By the time the market grows to a respectable size, it is already occupied by start-up companies that assumed the risk and found it rewarding early in the growth stage and that are now positioned as market leaders. "

An effective, user-centric innovation platform sheds those unnecessary pounds from the sumo-type companies. It allows a more agile and cost-effective approach to innovation. This ability will allow sumo-like companies to capitalize on ideas earlier in their market evolutions and not wait until the market matures. With lower costs and a faster ability to pursue new ideas, some of the traditional pounds that are slowing innovation in large companies are no longer relevant. Companies can now pursue emerging markets easily and justify the required investment because the investment required is much lower because of the shared innovation platform. As such, technology truly accelerates change because it facilitates faster acceptance and participation in new markets that until now were not part of the company's agenda.

JUST IMAGINE: FROM THE VENDOR'S IMAGINATION TO A USER'S IMAGINATION

In the world of technology, the imagination role was kept for the select few engineers who came up with earth-shattering, innovative products. IT usually played the role of compliant recipients who pay for the great innovations. A culture of genius engineers who started companies with a vision to change the world (and make billions in the process) is common in technology. As part of this culture, IT got used to playing a relatively passive role. The imagination of great new technology belonged by and large to the engineers, who often resented customers telling them what to do and how to code. As the creators of great ideas and the next new thing, they often assumed that they knew better than their customers.

Some will argue that the myriad of technology vendors' user groups and customer visits should substantiate the commitment to the customers.

Still, most of the customer insight that was collected was incremental. "I need another report," "Why don't you translate it to Chinese?" or "How about another field in the database?" is the traditional scope of the requirements. Others might argue that the home-grown systems are proof of the IT capacity for imagination. I too

> 66 *Some will argue that the myriad of technology vendors' user groups and customer visits should substantiate the commitment to the customers.* 99

would reject this notion because most of the home-grown applications are merely a duplication of traditional enterprise applications, such as ERP, that were highly modified to suit a certain complicated industry or company.

By and large, the imagination role was left to vendors. They would supply a set of well-defined and -coded applications and would recommend that IT adapt internal processes accordingly. At best, IT imagination was limited to changing internal processes to fit their newly acquired technologies, annoying users in the process.

With the innovation platform, a substantial change in roles takes place. Vendors no longer dictate the internal processes and the way to conduct business through their applications. The innovation platform shifts the imagination responsibility back to the organization in general and to IT in particular. The ability to create composite applications that are customized to an organization's special needs (but not yet as costly as home-grown applications because they leverage an existing platform) position IT in a new role.

Following years of blaming their application vendors for inflexibility and paying millions to adapt generic applications to their organization's specific needs, IT now starts with a clean piece of paper. They need to start with the process and strategy and then design their technologies to support them. It is now the role of IT, and not vendors, to come up with new ideas and wrap the technologies around it.

If in the past IT purchased complete, ready-to-hang pictures that were designed by artists, now the innovation platform provides them with all the tools required for a great picture. The paint and the brushes and the canvas are waiting for them. Only the artist is missing. If IT professionals look in the mirror, they will discover the artist. The long-requested flexibility has arrived. The innovation platform will deliver the ultimate flexibility. But it comes with a price: a new responsibility to imagine and create applications that fit users' experiences, behaviors, and ways of making decisions and doing business.

The growth in open source technology is ushering in the era of specialization and customization. The success of Linux was only one testimony, followed by several other traditional application companies that elected to follow the open source route. By providing their applications as an open source, they shift the imagination responsibility to the IT people. The open source trend requires IT professionals to consider users' needs first and then design applications accordingly. It ushered in thousands, if not millions, of variations, each modified to suit a business-specific function. Unlike home-grown applications that are designed from scratch for specialization and then are costly to maintain and upgrade, open source applications delivered a different promise. The open source applications and tools delivered the ultimate flexibility because IT did not work out an application from scratch, but instead utilized a common platform. This common platform accelerates design, enables endless mutations to be created, and reduces development and implementation costs.

But open source is a blessing in disguise. It is a blessing for those IT professionals who are willing to assume the newly bestowed responsibility of creating the applications they need, the way they are needed. It is a curse for those who are comfortable in the old way of doing things where the application vendors dictated the agenda and the business aligned itself accordingly.

In the future, every company's composite applications will be as different and as unique as the company's own identity and operation. The applications will be an expression of the way users do business. Users will not be subservient to a process that was designed for them by outsiders. Users will not have to adapt to the applications. Applications will wrap themselves around users and their behaviors. Users will then bear the primary role, with all the responsibilities associated with it, and will design applications accordingly. But, as unique as those applications will be, they will also share a strong commonality, the innovation platform that enabled them to be created.

The innovation platform shifted the role of imagination and application creation to users. IT, as a representative and as a user-centric function, will have to assume the new role and start imagining. If information-driven innovation is embraced, it will consist of millions of flexible applications as unique as the ideas they support and enable users to drive innovation to market faster.

10

The ROI Myth: How to Make a Real Business Impact

"The great end of life is not knowledge but action."

Thomas Henry Huxley

THE TRUTH BEHIND THE NUMBERS

Most IT organizations measure their success by their uptime and server availability. They are proud to present their "always on" programs, which allow users access to technologies, the Internet, or applications at any given time. Measured by such factors as the number of help desk complaints and problem resolution, IT digs its own grave. All these traditional measurements are cost related and make no evaluation of the real impact IT has on the business. By sticking religiously to these measurements, IT positions itself as a utility function rather than as an enabler of innovation and business success.

It is the success in achieving these measurements that blinds IT to its declining role and relevance to the corporate agenda. As part of the shift toward a user-centric model, IT must adapt its measurements and success factors. IT must adapt measurement factors that reflect the business success and user utilization of the information produced rather than focus on churning information. As a responsible producer of a product—information—IT ought to be measured by user acceptance and not by placing products on the shelf or in inventory, such as self service. Only users' actions can determine its true success. Although the old measures are important, they are taken for granted and assumed to be provided. As such, they ought to take a secondary place to the primary measurement factors around users' actions.

> " *IT must adapt measurement factors that reflect the business success and user utilization of the information produced rather than focus on churning information.* "

USERS' ACTION MEASUREMENT

IT will have to develop and track its performance through new tools and methods. Following users' behavior and utilization, IT will have to measure itself by factors that indicate user acceptance and the level of satisfaction provided by the information. The tools and measurement methods should be able to answer these questions:

- What is the most often used information?
- What are the trends of usage?
- Which users most often take advantage of the information?
- What is the information being used for?
- What is the level of satisfaction derived from the information?
- How are the quality and completeness of the information being perceived by its users?
- What information should be returned?
- What methods of consumption are the most popular?
- Which decisions have taken advantage of the information?
- What is the business impact the information-driven decisions have enabled?

Additionally, the following factors should be included in the new user-centric measurements IT uses:

- An increase in information usage
- An increase in innovative ideas and process introduction
- A reduction in time to market of new ideas
- A reduction in the cost of new idea assessment
- A reduction in innovation implementation costs
- The number of new composite applications
- An increase in the number of collaborative sessions
- An increase in the number of participating users
- A decrease in the time to value of innovation
- A decrease in innovation global rollout

What makes these factors different is that they are not based on abstract, non-user-related measures, such as network availability or uptime. The proposed new factors measure the results of user interactions with information. They focus on user actions, not on information availability. Many IT professionals will rush to reject these arguments and claim that they are related to issues outside their direct control. The argument that these measures are dependent on factors other than the innovation platform's availability and the information supporting the decisions may be partially true. Still, IT needs to connect itself and refine the ways in which it measures its contribution and successes through those new prisms and lenses of business results.

As IT professionals adapt to these measures, they will find better, fine-tuned ways to obtain more accurate information and raise their contributions to the decision process and innovation. But they ought to start placing themselves on the road to business and user-centric measurements.

By following a user segmentation model, the answers to these questions should be evaluated as per-customer segments. Each segment's success should be assessed based on its specific requirements and needs. Resources to address the gaps should then be allocated in accordance with the customer segments and not based on the traditional, "noisiest" user.

The proposed user action measurements will pose a challenge for IT, but it will operationalize any claim to become more focused on customers. As employees follow the factors that are being measured, and by focusing IT's measurements around the proposed factors, CIOs will send a clear message to their organizations that becoming customer-centric is not a slogan on a T-shirt, but is instead a new way of doing business. It sends a clear message that this is not just another program to be implemented on top of what IT professionals now do during their non-existent spare time. This strategy is a new one.

A NEW MANAGEMENT PRISM

Assuming accountability for customer action measurements will provide IT with a new prism in which to look at its place in an organization. The new measurements will broaden the scope of IT responsibility. IT will convert from tools provider to customer-satisfaction provider. This broader scope will bring IT closer to a business value provider model rather than a utility provider model. No longer the "gadget manager," IT will mature to become a business partner. Being measured on success rather than on capability will allow IT to become part of the core of its business because it will be measured by the same measurements as the business is measured.

> **" Assuming accountability for customer action measurements will provide IT with a new prism in which to look at its place in an organization. "**

These new business measurements will come with a price. They will require the reconsideration of many of the basics. The measurements will drive adaptation of the core competency and value proposition. Information will be transformed from "something we do" to "something they use." IT will shift its definition from the perspective of the tools it manages to the perspective of its users' actions. This is the ultimate business definition.

Utilization, not production, will be the battleground IT will have to win. It will force IT to integrate further with the organization and to stop seeing it as a set of processes operated by human robots. It will provide the view of the organization as a group of smart, creative, and innovative people who need tools in order to execute their ideas.

This shift in prism should not be looked on as a matter of semantics. It is a different way to conduct business. It is a way to free the creative human spirit and allow execution accordingly. It is about maximizing the human capital of the organization. It is the number-one challenge of every CEO. If IT will connect to it and help address it, IT will belong in the organization's mainstream agenda.

11

From Enforcer to Innovation Driver: The New Role of the Chief Information-to-Innovation Officer

"He whose deeds exceed his wisdom, his wisdom shall endure; but he whose wisdom exceed his deeds, his wisdom will not endure."

Talmud

ASSUMING A NEW ROLE

As IT adapts to a user-centric, growth-driven model, a new IT leadership role is being defined. CIOs need to reconsider their roles and responsibilities and reshape them in accordance with the innovation

> " *Declaring innovation as the focus is not and should not be treated as a slogan or a communication program. It is a fundamental change in the IT mission, core competency, and value proposition.* "

focus. Declaring innovation as the focus is not and should not be treated as a slogan or a communication program. It is a fundamental change in the IT mission, core competency, and value proposition.

At the heart of the CIO transformation is the transformation of the core competency. CIOs will have to take a good, hard look at what defines them and their operations today and ask whether those core competencies are worth keeping. Will those core competencies keep the operation at the cutting edge of the business's agenda? How many of those core competencies are becoming commodities, ready to be relinquished to make room for new core competencies? Often, it is fear of the unknown and a lack of experience that pushes people back to the warm and cozy environment of the known and familiar. They stick to "what worked so far" and assume that it will work forever. The transformation challenge is to not only recognize the new core competencies, but also overcome those natural fears.

Future CIOs need to evolve into a CI^2Os, or chief information-to-innovation officers. No longer acting as factory managers responsible for information production, CIOs will resemble marketers, focusing on users and their interactions with their product: information. It is that chemistry between users and information that defines the evolving CI^2O. The existence of the information and its availability will no longer be sufficient. They become a utility, like services, with diminishing added value. At best, they are taken for granted; at worst, they are ignored. In fact, new CI^2Os will source the needed information from multiple sources, not all under their direct management and responsibility. Their focus will be satisfying users' needs, not producing their information. The old CIO definition of success was a lack of complaints. Silence from users was the best form of compliment. A CI^2O's definition of success will be appreciation and recognition caused by users achieving their business goals through information utilization.

To achieve this change, CI^2Os will have to form a migration path. Through the evolution process, they will have to chart a new path between their current production management positions and their future users' utilization responsibility. This path will include recognizing its new core competency and letting go of the old one. A focus on user innovation and organization growth will require shifting resources to assist users rather than produce for them. The value proposition is shifting from delivering information to ensuring its impact and usefulness. In designing the evolution path, CI^{2}Os need to consider these issues:

- **Chart a new path for technology utilization.** No direct link now exists between information production and information utilization. The virtue of producing information and managing networks does not lend itself naturally to understanding users. In fact, it often blinds information producers from understanding users, as described in the ecosystem analysis in Chapter 1. Building the bridge between the two distinctly different ecosystems is the first priority of an evolving CI^{2}O. Understanding the difference between these two ecosystems is already a first step in admitting that you cannot force one on top of the other; instead, they have to evolve. Ultimately, CI^{2}Os will have to plan for information utilization and managing users' experiences of information and technology.

- **Provide different services to different people.** Understanding user behavior and segmenting users based on their lifestyles, consumption patterns, and business impact will be critical to defining the user-centric model. It will provide an important insight to CI^{2}Os about who their users are beyond their employee IDs and how they want to be serviced. This shift will move from a one-size-fits-all model that is dominant in many production-focused IT organizations. It will also provide a shift in resource allocation because IT organizations will have to be aligned with the business impact of users, not their capacity to create "noise" in the system.

- **Connect to the business agenda.** CI^{2}Os need to start their assessments of their IT value propositions with their organizations' strategic goals and initiatives: Follow the money trail, and then redesign services accordingly. This reverse-engineering approach will ensure connection to business issues. Although many CIOs believe that they already have done so, their performance measurements and user opinions tell a different story. A

> " *CI^{2}Os need to start their assessments of their IT value propositions with their organizations' strategic goals and initiatives: Follow the money trail, and then redesign services accordingly.* "

reality check is in order to ensure that no disillusion distorts the reality as it is perceived by users. User reality, after all, dictates user behavior and utilization. If users perceive IT as disconnected, they disregard its information.

- **Reevaluate core competency.** With a heavy burden of 80 percent of IT budgets tied up in existing network infrastructure, hardware, desktops, and applications management, CI²Os can easily lose site of their core competency. Core competency in managing hardware quickly becomes a commodity that is outsourced to third-party vendors who claim greater economies of scale than IT can deliver internally. IT core competency ought to evolve around and focus on linking and integrating information with business decisions, as opposed to facilitating the tools that create information. It is the next natural evolution of information, and IT cannot trust users to do it on their own. Information integration into business processes, innovations, and decision making are the new core competencies of CI²Os.
- **Leverage cross-functional roles.** IT professionals and CIOs are in the unique position of being a cross-functional operation. As such, they get to see the complete picture of their companies. While sales and manufacturing often focus on their own domain, expertise, and narrow agendas, IT does not share the same flaw. It is free to see all functional operations in a company, to provide an insight for synergies and to facilitate cooperation and cross-functional leverage. To achieve that outcome, IT needs to evolve its role and be proactive about its information utilization. It is the complete ownership of information utilization that will drive IT to become more proactive and ensure the success of its information in an organization. This success, defined as integration into business decisions and the driving of innovation, will be highly dependent on cross-functional cooperation. This cooperation can be better facilitated by an operation that does not have a vested interest in narrow domain expertise and, as such, is free to present and cooperate around the complete picture. IT has this freedom, although it hardly takes advantage of it.

FROM INFORMATION PRODUCTION TO INFORMATION UTILIZATION

The shift from a production-based organization to an innovation-based organization is not just a matter of semantics. It is not something a CIO can add as a "sauce" on top of its current operation. It is fundamentally a different IT organization. It carries some significant change in function, core competency, and measurement. The table shown in Figure 11-1 details some required changes.

Production-based organization	Function	Innovation-based organization
Managing systems and services	Core competency	Integrating information and business decisions
Size of budget and number of people	Focus	Business impact
The cost crunchers/optimization	Impact	The business builders/revenue generation
Expenses — return on Investment	ROI	Revenues — return on Innovation
Information production factory	Mode of operation	Information utilization
Mass usage	Users	Business decision makers
Internal	Information sources	Multisource
Production	Information focus	Utilization
How to reduce costs	The questions	Why not? What if?

Figure 11-1. From Information Production to Information Utilization

As this figure indicates, becoming a growth driver through user-centric IT is not a trivial matter. It requires addressing the core of the IT operation. Some precious concerns will have to be abandoned to allow room for the new focus. One cannot simultaneously be production focused and user-centric. Those qualities are, as described in previous chapters, from distinctly different planets. IT professionals ought to choose on which planet they want to reside. Dual citizenship will be a recipe for a sort of schizophrenia, not clarity. Just as a dancer cannot dance both the tango and the waltz at the same time, an IT attempt to dance on both floors is doomed for failure.

> " *One cannot simultaneously be production focused and user-centric.* "

To usher in the new era of information utilization, information-driven innovation, and user-centricity, it is insufficient to declare a new IT agenda. Something old must go before the new arrives. CI²Os will not be able to conduct business as usual and run user-centricity on top of it. Their companies' IT professionals, busy with the firefighting mode completely occupied by their servers and storage management, do not have any additional capacity to add new tasks. They must be freed from some of their current tasks to be allowed to perform in accordance with the new IT agenda.

Outsourcing commodities such as utility function will be required in order to allow new thinking into an organization. Following outsourcing, "Less is more" needs to be adopted as a motto.

IT functions now focus on quantity of information. IT professionals are consumed by information production and, as discussed in Chapter 1, they confuse and drive inaction among their users. Less quantity and more quality information is required. Quality information will be determined based on the completeness, timeliness, relevance, and actionability of the information. The faster a user can make a decision with the information, the better the information quality is.

Redesigning the decision process to allow information to support users, rather than adapt users to the way processes and information were designed, is another aspect that ought to be addressed. Users will no longer tolerate being subservient to a system that was designed with them as an afterthought. Technology for the sake of technology will not take root in a user-centric model. Users and their behavior must come first, technology, second.

Change management should be built into the transformation. In this case, IT will face a dual challenge: transforming its own operations and employee behavior and transforming its users' perceptions. The two tasks are interdependent because one is geared toward servicing the other. Without users' embrace of this new IT role, all the internal changes will not deliver the innovation support that is required. Change management will be an important test for IT professionals' truly required sales capabilities, as discussed in Chapter 10. Selling their capabilities, willingness, and interest in supporting users and designing information around them will be at the core of the change management program.

CIOs who will choose to evolve will ensure their relevance in the organization. The evolution is not a matter of choice, but, rather, is a necessity—a necessity due to new CEO and business agendas and to changes within the IT world and how technology has evolved in the last two decades. But, even though determining this choice is a necessity, it is nevertheless a choice for CIOs to determine how to evolve their operations. This choice should determine the future of IT and its shape in years to come. More importantly, if the right choice is made, it might well determine the future of its whole organization and its ability to compete, innovate, and grow. This choice is in the hands of CIOs.

12

A New Agenda for Technology Vendors

"Experience is not what happens to you; it is what you do with what happens to you."

Aldous Huxley

THE TECHNOLOGIST'S TRAP: INNOVATION FOR THE SAKE OF INNOVATION

While working at HP, I can recall a discussion with a lab manager who, after expressing his frustration with a customer complaint, stated, "The customer is stupid." This statement irritated me. The lab manager complained that ignorant customers bothered him with useless, unfounded issues. I recall my response to the claim that the customer is stupid: "Somehow," I told the lab manager, "the products you produce, I only manage to sell to stupid customers. I do not know why, but this is the fact of life. The smart customers refuse to buy your developed products." It turned out that the customer was right.

This story illustrates a typical trap that technology vendors are facing: They have an aura of superiority, the notion that "we know better." Often, artists' behavior can be detected. They act as the sole owners of

115

their products and reluctantly allow customers to enjoy their handmade treasures. Defeating this dangerous attitude is the challenge of technology vendors. They have already gone a long way toward satisfying their customers: Engineers and product managers are visiting customers more often and seeking their insight on new features. Although vendors are now committed to finding out what their "stupid" customers want, they often fall into the trap of "knowing better" and assuming that they understood what customers "really" want. This situation often leads to customer-centric features that are too far from customers' original desires. It is exactly this attitude that in the past led many CIOs, frustrated with their vendors' inability to understand and act on their wishes, to default to home-grown solutions.

The gap between superior technologists and stupid customers is shrinking, but not fast enough. The initial distance was so great that the progress that was achieved is often not good enough.

Technology vendors, just like CIOs, will have to adapt and "wrap themselves around" their customers. Successful technology vendors of the future will learn to respect and accept customers as primary, not secondary, to their businesses. These vendors will assume a humble position toward customers, accepting them as true, intelligent partners and let go of the superiority complex. Customer insight will not be an oversight. It will be the *core* sight in their operations. Even technology advancements not forecasted or requested by customers will still go through the rigorous customer insight adaptation. Vendors who will internalize and execute according to the principle that the customer, and not the technology, is their core competency will win.

> " Successful technology vendors of the future will learn to respect and accept customers as primary, not secondary, to their businesses. "

DEEP DISCOUNTING IS NOT A STRATEGY

For the past couple of years, technology vendors developed a unique core competency: deep discounting. Failing to innovate and operating under significant competitive pressures, many succumbed to heavy discounting as a strategic measure. Theses discounts only further diluted their value to customers, who no longer could assign a true value to the products. While chasing the 800–pound-gorilla position, many technology vendors failed to focus on value and instead developed unique skills in dropping their prices at the sight of a competitive offer.

The winners of the future race will be those who can understand the true value of their wares in the eyes of their customers. It is the failure to do this that led many vendors to the downward spiral of the discounting game. In addition, with the further segmentation of value between vendors, channel partners, integrators, and internal IT people, the total value proposition of a certain solution was too fragmented. When such fragmentation occurs, customers are left to assemble the complete value proposition. This assembly has a cost associated with it. The rule of thumb is that the one who assembles all components of the value proposition is keeping the premium price. A vendor who delivers a complete, total solution keeps a premium price because the customer saves time and money and the time to value is shorter. Customers who are left to do the assembly and manage a project will apply the costs of time, resources, and

> **" A vendor who delivers a complete, total solution keeps a premium price because the customer saves time and money and the time to value is shorter. "**

delayed time to value to the price they are willing to pay for the technology. As such, they will keep the premium and pay the absolute minimum necessary. Discounting will play a major role in such a situation.

Although technology vendors focus their efforts on the features delivered, customers often find this presentation useless. The uselessness of the presentation comes in two primary ways: a feature set that is too rich and an implementation nightmare. IT organizations are usually aware of available feature sets. Their needs constitute a mere fraction of the complete set of features offered by vendors. They are trying to sell customers a package deal of features, many of which they do not need or will never use. Just like the long list of fonts in word processing software that most users never bother to try out, the feature sets in many technologies are too overwhelming and destined to be ignored. Therefore, demonstrating so many packaged features is not delivering the right message. Often, it sends the opposite message: "We do not need all those features." While technology vendors are focusing on their features demonstration, customers are fearing the implementation nightmare. They have "been there" many times over. Technology prices ballooned because of exorbitant implementation costs. Customers are not looking for features assurance; they are seeking assurance around implementation and its timeframe and costs. Most vendors stay vague when discussing this matter, if not ignoring it altogether.

Failing to address real customer issues, combined with leaving so much of the value proposition for others to deliver, resulted in partial and therefore unclear value. Discounted pricing reflected that fragmentation.

It is time to embrace the value and enhance it rather than dilute it. It is time for technology vendors to reconsider their total value and assume complete ownership of value to their customers. Winners in the future will focus not on bundling features, but, rather, on trying to sell more for less. Future winners will sell customers what they need. They will ensure success in implementation and usage and not stay at the license-fee level.

BUILDING BUSINESS VALUE

Winners of the future will focus not on technology sales, but, rather, on results sales. Although dependent on users to achieve complete success, technology vendors will select customers who are the most likely to succeed, rather than sell to the masses and focus all their efforts on ensuring their complete success in achieving their goals. The goals to be achieved are not technology goals, such as installations and on-time training; rather, they are driving innovation and business objectives, justifying the technology implementation, and usage.

> " Although dependent on users to achieve complete success, technology vendors will select customers who are the most likely to succeed, rather than sell to the masses and focus all their efforts on ensuring their complete success in achieving their goals. "

To achieve complete ownership of success, companies will have to focus on several new criteria:

- **Assemble and sell complete values.** To win in the future, technology vendors will assume complete responsibility for their value and not leave it to third parties to do their job. This confusing and fragmented system leaves too much money on the table. It also has developed an effective culture of finger pointing and partial responsibility, which often means none at all. Future winners will focus on the complete assembly of their value propositions to win the larger share of customer budgets and premium prices. A complete assembly will allow faster time to value, which will justify customer efforts and lower total cost of ownership. To achieve these goals, technology vendors will first have to understand what a complete solution means from the IT perspective. Some of the new tasks of CI²Os, as described in Chapter 11, will already provide an insight into what complete solutions will look like in the future. Only after vendors get a grasp on the new definition of complete solutions will they be able to redesign the total value proposition to match evolving expectations and deliver them to customers.

- **Own the complete dissemination of tools and solution.** The word *complete* should be redefined for those who seek future success. *Complete* will win beyond just application training and customization of a few reports. *Complete* will mean assuming responsibility and measuring success through business objectives, not technology objectives. Fast availability of applications and capabilities is no longer sufficient. Ensuring that users see the value and utilizing it in a strategic context are crucial. To achieve this level of success, training and strategic capabilities must be added to the overall portfolio. These capabilities will assist IT in selling the solution and explaining it from a strategic, rather than capability, standpoint. Future winners will include strategic and utilization capabilities to best position their solutions and achieve promised business results.

- **Take ownership of ROI.** For years, vendors assisted their customers in determining the return on investment associated with their technologies. The numbers were always impressive and made the decision easy and almost a no-brainer. But, following the technology implementation, few customers were able to demonstrate the promised measured results. The reasons vary from customers not complying with required changes to exaggerated, unrealistic expectations. Vendors were often reluctant to guarantee results and claimed that they had no control over the complete execution of the projects and that technology played a partial role in the promised return on investment. Winners in the future will assume that responsibility. By building tools into their technology to track and report the promised return on investment, vendors will embed business results measurement tools in their technology to demonstrate promised results to customers. Following up with customers beyond the technology implementation and making sure that the project is on track and delivers as promised will become an integral sales process that will not end only at the technology implementation level. The ownership to deliver promised results will be shifted from IT professionals and their organizations to vendors. This shift is not an apologetic one that attempts to justify their value. Rather, it is the vendors' opportunity to connect and be an integral part of the businesses and to shift from tools providers to value drivers. To do so, vendors ought to assume greater responsibility and a commitment to success.

- **Participate in results-based selling.** User-based and network-based pricing will become obsolete. Today's technology pricing does not reflect value. It is an odd representation combining competitive pricing pressures and invalidated assumptions of what the market can bear. None of it has anything to do with the value provided to customers. To avoid the fate of utility, technology vendors will have to adapt to a utility-and-results model. Customers will shift to vendors all responsibility for the costs of implementation, and vendors will be compensated by a better price based on results delivered. While assuming the upfront costs, vendors will also have to ensure success. The reward, however, will be significantly higher than the out-of-context pricing offered today.

DARING TO SHARE THE RISK

Future winners will assume greater risk, but will be rewarded accordingly. By delivering a complete value and not sharing it with others, vendors will be required to add new capabilities to their portfolios and to invest further in the completeness of their solutions. The dissemination process might take longer and will require additional new resources, both of which require investment. Results-based pricing will further payments to the business results achievements timeframe, as opposed to the installation timeframe. All these factors will pose an additional risk for vendors. But they will bear a greater reward. Obtaining payment based on driving results will ensure the ultimate match of vendors, technologies, and business needs. The tools will reflect their true value to customers and not just an arbitrary price. This approach, however, will require some courage. The current system is comfortable and familiar. Vendors will be reluctant to change and will attempt to minimize their risk. It will also be

> **" Future winners will assume greater risk, but will be rewarded accordingly. "**

safe to assume that customers might be reluctant to be held responsible to their end of the bargain. Why would they want to buy at the real value if prices are continually decreasing? By providing complete value, including redefining the concept of completeness and accelerating time to value, vendors will be entitled to a true reflection of the value they have delivered. Wrapping their value propositions around a business and placing users at the heart of their core competencies bear the potential of significant reward to those who dare to do it.

13

Information-Driven Innovation

"The man without imagination has no wings, he cannot fly."

Muhammad Ali

TRANSFORMING INFORMATION'S VALUE

For generations, innovative technology made the world progress in leaps and bounds and ushered in new eras. Technology played, and is still playing, an important role in the future of organizations and transforming them into cost-efficient, labor-reduced operations. Those capabilities, however, are becoming commodities. Cost cutting is not a long-term strategy. IT functions cannot count on such a strategy to justify their resources and activities, either. Growth through innovation is the focus of every organization, even if, in parallel, some cost-cutting measures will be conducted. Cost cutting is often associated with survival mode and is not expected to sustain a business for the long run. Those cost-reduction activities should not be confused with the mainstream agenda and core competency of a business: growth.

In his book *Does IT Matter?*, Nick Carr argues that IT is inevitably going the way of other utilities, such as electricity, telephone, and

> " Cost cutting is often associated with survival mode and is not expected to sustain a business for the long run. "

railroads. IT, he argues, becomes an irrelevant commodity that from a strategic standpoint is invisible. Carr may be right, but only if IT will allow him to be right. Although some IT functions, such as Internet access, are becoming commodities and are being taken for granted by users, it does not have to be that way. If IT will continue to focus on cost crunching, it will accelerate its descent to the commoditization abyss. If IT will connect to the main engine of the company, growth through innovation, it will avoid this fate.

The future of technology lies in enabling growth, in supporting the core of the business and not operating in marginal survival mode. Many companies can relatively easily reduce costs and find ways to save money. Fewer companies, however, have a systematic way to grow their businesses through innovative products, processes, and programs. Many companies are experts in following market trends and do what everyone else is doing: Ensure their destiny in commoditization. Few companies have the courage and knowledge to break their industry rules and chart a new path in which to lead. Following trends focuses on performing, and acting on, someone else's agenda. The rewards, the leftovers of the leader, are meager. Creating new rules is about creating new rewards. It is about strengthening your core competency and enhancing it. It is about providing customers with a new promise and obtaining a premium price and loyalty for it.

For many people, innovation is the domain of a few scientists. Innovation is quickly associated with inspiration, a form of incidental discovery.

> " In reality, innovation is by far more about hard work than about inspiration and incidental discoveries. "

Companies cannot allow themselves to be so highly dependent on a few geniuses or the possibility of unpredictable incidents. In reality, innovation is by far more about hard work than about inspiration and incidental discoveries. Companies ought to distribute the responsibility among all their stakeholders, internal and external. They ought to democratize the innovation process and allow every customer, supplier, and employee to contribute to the innovation process. This process consists of mass innovation created by the masses. In it, individuals come before technology. Complementing the focus on users, innovation is, and ought to be, about the systematic pursuit of opportunism and is a method to execute it successfully. It is about doing hard work and having a set of tools to assist users to achieve it.

Building a systematic innovation mechanism into every organization is highly dependent on having information. Especially when innovation is democratized, information plays a crucial role across the complete innovation process, from idea collection and the prioritization of different ideas to supporting decisions concerning which ideas to purse. Additionally, in innovation creation, information should provide guidance to budgetary and manufacturing processes to ensure faster, smoother, and cost-effective creation. During business realization, information again plays a role in supporting go-to-market plans and in maximizing innovative product or service revenues. Information should play a greater role in what seems to be an intuitive and unreliable process. By complementing the emotional, gut-feeling nature of people's behavior, information can assist companies in not only making decisions, but also achieving intelligent, commercial-driven decisions.

Redefining his or her role is the challenge of every IT person. Several trends are colliding to create the perfect storm. From outsourcing pressures to information overflow, from unrealized ROI to the shift of budgets in business units, the IT role of cost cruncher, or even network access manager, is being challenged. The void in innovation as a systematic mechanism to drive growth and the connection to the information creation process best positions IT to respond to the challenge.

Creating an innovation platform that allows the ongoing collection, assessment, and implementation of innovation is an enterprise-wide challenge. As experts in technology and as owners of the information product, IT is best positioned to tackle this challenge. By shifting their focus from the current mode of cost reduction and measuring success through uptime, IT professionals will start their journey toward full integration with the business agenda by connecting themselves to the mainstream concern of every CEO. This change will require shifting the focus from server and storage capabilities to integrating information

> " By shifting their focus from the current mode of cost reduction and measuring success through uptime, IT professionals will start their journey toward full integration with the business agenda by connecting themselves to the mainstream concern of every CEO. "

with the business decision process. Assuming that the innovation cycle will provide IT with a sustainable platform and responsibility that are not subject to the outsourcing threat, it will build a respectable, long-term role for CIOs and their teams.

As Figure 13-1 indicates, information plays a crucial role in every step of the innovation cycle. To support decisions and provide execution guidance, an innovation platform ought to be created. Because the innovation platform is user-centric, it will revolve around users and their access and privileges. The platform will provide users with information integration that gives them fast access to wide sources of information, to allow better assessments and decisions. Combined with knowledge management and business intelligence, the platform will allow users to better utilize information and make intelligent decisions. Combined with collaborative tools and the ability to create tools and applications easily, the innovation platform will allow ideas that yesterday were deemed not feasible because of costs or knowledge, but will be tomorrow's blockbusters.

Assuming responsibility for the innovation cycle and platform will require IT to complete several changes. This new responsibility will require a shift toward a redefinition of the IT focus and core competency. As information producers, they will need to assume responsibility for information utilization. IT will no longer be able to count on users to do their parts. It will have to be actively involved in it, in order to enhance users' effectiveness. Creating a user-centric model is the next required change. Today, many IT systems are designed from the process standpoint. In an innovation model, these systems will be designed around users. Users and their behavior, not engineers with cool ideas detached from their users, will dictate the way technology will be designed. The new role in innovation facilitation will shift the imagination responsibility from vendors to IT. IT will now have to come up with the requirements and design applications accordingly. This task is

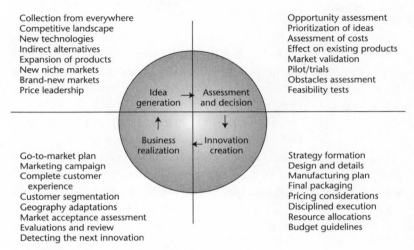

The innovation cycle —
Information-driven innovation

Collection from everywhere
Competitive landscape
New technologies
Indirect alternatives
Expansion of products
New niche markets
Brand-new markets
Price leadership

Opportunity assessment
Prioritization of ideas
Assessment of costs
Effect on existing products
Market validation
Pilot/trials
Obstacles assessment
Feasibility tests

Idea generation → Assessment and decision

Business realization ← Innovation creation

Go-to-market plan
Marketing campaign
Complete customer
  experience
Customer segmentation
Geography adaptations
Market acceptance assessment
Evaluations and review
Detecting the next innovation

Strategy formation
Design and details
Manufacturing plan
Final packaging
Pricing considerations
Disciplined execution
Resource allocations
Budget guidelines

Figure 13-1. Information–Driven Innovation

not a return to the home–grown application days; it consists of leveraging an existing platform that allows quick, flexible, and sometimes disposable applications to support a project and program or a function.

When the ownership of information and customer-centricity are regarded as the focal points of the new CI^{2}O, these points need to be put into the proper context. The ownership of users and information entails ownership of the processes. IT is no longer just a set of tools, but is also the enabler and owner of the business processes. At the juncture between users and information is the business process, or the ability to execute. It is in this business process ownership context that IT needs to view its new role. It must embrace the bigger picture of business process ownership, which is greater than servicing people and delivering information. The essence of information is its utilization and execution by people making

> **" At the juncture between users and information is the business process, or the ability to execute. It is in this business process ownership context that IT needs to view its new role. "**

decisions (one form of business process) or by operations (another form of business process). IT should not stop short of the complete utilization ownership and the assurance that users will be able to execute business processes easily and quickly.

Innovation is discussed often and agreed on in many companies. No one is challenging the need for it. Few companies will admit that they do not do it. But fewer can demonstrate a consistent mechanism to facilitate and nurture it. Innovation ought to move from lip service that is paid to an execution stage. IT, with its expertise, can assist in it and complement users and empower them to make more and better decisions that usher more ideas into commercial innovative success.

By empowering users with the right tools and ensuring their usage through decision process redesign, IT can accelerate change and allow users and companies to take calculated and well-designed risks that will allow new innovation to be introduced in the market. Following years of cost-cutting expertise, growth is back in fashion. In reality, it was never out of fashion—it was merely at a stage in which companies forgot how to innovate and were more comfortable flexing their cost-reduction muscles. The growth-through-innovation requirement was always on the agenda—it simply received a lower priority. Those who knew how to consistently deliver it were able to do so even during tough times. They grew their businesses and are in a better position to capitalize on market growth. Those who were having a random, unplanned affair with innovation and growth focused their efforts on shrinking their budgets and becoming less competitive.

The argument for growth and innovation as a systematic mechanism and the utilization of information as an enabler is not time related. The innovation platform and the innovation cycle ought to be created and managed every day. IT should assume the responsibility and become both the innovation driver, through its information, and the change accelerator.

Individuals are at the core of the innovation process. It is time for tools to support individuals rather than to be subservient to them.

Beyond the need for hard proof for innovation and growth, another important factor is often neglected. It is a soft factor that most companies do not know how to measure or treat. Although this book addresses the value of the user-centric model from the perspective of market share growth, business growth, and innovation, another important aspect ought to be mentioned: employee readiness. Unhappy, hassled users cannot come up with innovative ideas. If they are convinced that their companies do not care about them; if they feel like a small screw in a huge process; if they are convinced that their companies are not delivering the tools to help them work effectively, they will divert their minds from thinking in an innovative fashion. They simply will not feel like doing it. They will be too upset or resentful to contribute in a creative way.

Most companies are aware of this emotional aspect of users, but are unsure what to do with it. A user-centric model combined with an innovation platform that makes users collaborate, innovate, and execute faster will contribute to employees' emotional factor. It will send a clear signal that a company is user-centric, not self-centric. By making the effort to place users as a first priority, companies will encourage their users to reciprocate and deliver their best efforts. If IT redesigns itself to fit users' needs and make them the center of all their work, it will nurture the innovative spirit within users and assist companies in creating more ideas and, ultimately, more winning products and services.

> *" By making the effort to place users as a first priority, companies will encourage their users to reciprocate and deliver their best efforts. "*

Creating and managing the innovation platform will enable IT to deliver a powerful tool that is as agile as users are, not as rigid as processes are. The platform runs at the pace of ideas, instead of slowing them down, and allows organizations to keep pace and leap beyond the market's conditions and trends toward the creation of brand-new trends that the companies lead. It is a powerful promise that technology did not previously deliver. At best, it allows markets and industry to arrive together at the next level. All competitors ultimately achieve parity. Because applications deliver the same functionality to all, with the ability to deliver unique applications (as unique as the individual's ideas), companies can then differentiate and pursue rule-breaking strategies that they were barred from earlier because of technological limitations. It is a true transformation that IT should embrace. Technology truly adapts to users and their companies' cultures and business DNA as opposed to being subservient to them and to their way of thinking and doing business. It is about freely unleashing visions and ideas of the companies rather than the vendors. This is the ultimate freedom to innovate through the human spirit and creativity, empowered by information to create commercial success.

Resources and Background Material

Chabrow, E. CEOs Say Revenue Growth Is More Important Than Cost-Cutting. *Information Week*. February 2004.

CIO Insight research study. Business Intelligence. *CIO Insight*, May 2003.

CIO Insight research study. The Future of IT. *CIO Insight*, January 2004.

CIO Insight research study. IT Spending: Are You Spending Enough? *CIO Insight*, February 2004.

CIO Insight research study. Leadership. *CIO Insight*, October 2003.

CIO Insight research study. The Real-Time Enterprise. *CIO Insight*, July 2003.

CIO Insight research study. The Role of the CIO. *CIO Insight*, January 2004.

Computer Language Company, Inc. *Computer Desktop Encyclopedia*, 1981–2003.

Feld, C.S., Stoddard, D.B. Getting IT Right. *Harvard Business Review*. February 2004: 72–79.

Grove, A. Churning Things Up. *Fortune*. August 2003: 59–61.

Hamel, G. When Dinosaurs Mate. *The Wall Street Journal* (online). January 2004.

Hammer, M. Deep Change: How Operational Innovation Can Transform Your Company. *Harvard Business Review*. April 2004: 84–93.

Hawn, C. If He's So Smart . . . Steve Jobs, Apple, and the Limits of Innovation. *Fast Company* 78. January 2004: 68–76.

Hill, D. Rational mind, emotions connect for decisions. *Marketing News*. September 2003.

Houghton Mifflin Company. *The American Heritage Dictionary of the English Language*, Fourth Edition, 2003.

Joachim, D. We Asked, You Told. Second annual reader survey. *Network Computing*. October 2003: 35–47.

Melymuka, K. IT-Driven Innovation at Whirlpool. Computerworld. February 2004.

Rasenberger, J. *High Steel: The Daring Men Who Built the World's Greatest Skyline.* HarperCollins, 2004.

Schrage, M. Daniel Kahneman: The Thought Leader Interview. strategy+business 33. Winter 2003: 121–125.

Simpson, J.B. *Simpson's Contemporary Quotations.* Houghton Mifflin, 1988.

Strategos innovation survey. www.strategos.com.

Treacy, M., Sims, J., Lieberman, G. Real Returns on R&D. *Optimize,* March 2003.

Tuchman, B. *The March of Folly: From Troy to Vietnam.* New York: Knopf, 1984.

Index

131

Notes

Notes

Notes

Notes

Notes

Notes

About the Author

Lior Arussy is an author, visionary, and creative catalyst. He is the president of Strativity Group, a customer experience management research and advisory firm working with Global 2000 clients. His syndicated column, *Focus: Customer,* reaches more than 250,000 readers worldwide every month. In addition, he is the author of four books, including *The Experience! How to Wow Your Customer and Create a Passionate Workplace* (CMP Books, 2002). In addition, he has published more than 50 articles, including an article in *Harvard Business Review,* in publications around the world.

For his thought leadership and contribution to the industry, Arussy received the 2003 Influential Leaders award from *CRM* magazine.

About Strativity Group

S trativity Group, Inc., is a global research and advisory firm advising organizations on how to create lasting, profitable relationships with their customers and employees by transforming strategies and their execution to revolve around the customer experience. The company provides brainstorming workshops, training sessions, and consulting services assisting organizations in making the transformation toward a customer-centric business model.

Strativity Group, Inc., works with both Global 2000 companies and emerging businesses around the world. Its clients include SAP, Honeywell, Computer Associates, American Management Association, Seagate Technology, Jacada, and DVTel.

STRATIVITY
For more information contact info@strativitygroup.com or point your browser to www.StrativityGroup.com.